LIVING WISDOM

THE
SACRED EARTH

BRIAN LEIGH MOLYNEAUX

SERIES CONSULTANT: **PIERS VITEBSKY**

MACMILLAN

IN ASSOCIATION WITH
DUNCAN BAIRD PUBLISHERS

The Sacred Earth

First published in Great Britain in 1995

A DBP book
published by
Macmillan Reference Books
a division of Macmillan
Publishers Limited
Cavaye Place
London SW10 9PG
and Basingstoke

A CIP catalogue record for this book is available from the British Library

ISBN 0-333-63849-2

Conceived, created and designed by
Duncan Baird Publishers
Sixth Floor
Castle House
75–76 Wells Street
London W1P 3RE

10 9 8 7 6 5 4 3 2 1

Editors: Rachel Storm, Peter Bently
Designer: Karen Wilks
Picture research: Jan Croot
Cartographic Design:
Line + Line

Typset in Times NR MT
Colour reproduction by
Colourscan, Singapore
Printed in Singapore

Contents

Introduction

The expanse of the Namib Desert in Nambia has more visual affinities with the sea than with many places on Earth. Often, arid inland landscapes are said in local folk metaphor to "dream of the sea".

Since prehistoric times, humankind in many cultures of the world has had a dynamic relationship with the Earth as a living, nurturing body, a sacred source of vitality. Images and materials of the Earth have been used to make sense of life. For the Aboriginal peoples of Australia, the landscape has been drawn into a complex system of interconnecting social and religious beliefs, informed by the idea of the Dreaming – the time beyond memory when ancestral beings roamed the land, forming its features. Elsewhere (for example, in the Shinto beliefs of Japan), rocks, trees, rivers and other aspects of the natural world have been seen as deeply invested with spirit life, perhaps as a way to account for the teeming otherness of natural phenomena. Additionally, many belief systems accommodate a view of the Earth and its flora and fauna as material for the myth-making impulse, whose function may be interpreted as a means of coming to terms with the mysteries of birth, life and death, and other fundamental human experiences.

Since the rise of Newtonian science in the West, the balanced relationship between humankind and the living world has come under threat. Global warming and the loss of rainforest are planetary *causes célèbres*. In a scientific context, the new, conservationist picture of nature's infinite variety is encapsulated by the term "biodiversity". Yet alongside the scientific defence of the planet, there is currently a broad movement of sympathy, across the West, for the ancient wisdoms of a broad range of cultures, from the astronomical preoccupations of Mesoamerica to the shamanistic beliefs of the Amazon basin, Siberia and the Arctic. In a sense, this movement reverses the orthodox position of popular Western thinking with regard to science and the supernatural: science becomes the object of scepticism, while mysteries ("Earth mysteries", in the fashionable idiom) acquire new credibility, inspiring a quest for understanding in spirit (while recognizing the limitations of *cognitive* understanding) such enigmatic phenomena as the prehistoric stone monuments of Britain, the Paleolithic cave paintings of southern France and northern Spain, and the medicine wheels of the plains of North America.

No longer do we elevate inventiveness to quasi-divine status or celebrate technology as a benefit in itself. Increasingly, we attach greater importance to a true sense of our place in the scheme of things, and this has recently become a theme of the new science, with its emphasis on time and cosmic origins, and the dizzying paradox of the Uncertainty Principle.

Technology has separated many billions of people from the natural world by distancing them from basic resources: electricity reaches us through a wire, food comes to us dressed and wrapped. Such separation has made it difficult for people to appreciate the influence of nature on their lives. However, it has been argued that religions, just as much as science, have played a part in skewing the relationship between humankind and the natural world. The displacement of an ancient, universal, nurturing mother (nature) goddess by male sky gods (symbolized by the victory of the god Apollo over the serpent Python at Delphi, the navel of the world) has been used as an argument in the feminist attack on patriarchal societies. An often repeated extension of this argument is that the most influential religions of the historical era have contributed to the damage by focusing on a single, supreme sky god, separate from creation.

At the most prosaic and secular level, the landscape is widely seen in the West as having a calming influence, correcting urban perspectives, adjusting our eyes to the long view. Walking, a simple and universal occupation, re-introduces us to old rhythms and expectations far removed from those of the modernized world with its four-minute attention span. A similar, but more profound and more challenging, adjustment comes about when we look in a spirit of intelligent open-minded inquiry at the sacred meanings imposed upon the landscape by various cultures that are foreign to us in time or space. The mysteries of the Earth are transmitted in images, structures, texts and oral traditions that enshrine a wealth of myths, rituals and religious beliefs. In approaching these sources, we feel our imagination open up under the influence of ideas that will always lie just beyond the reach of the intellect – profound ideas to which we are tempted to apply the term "truths" because they move us to champion their instinctual validity. Engaging with them, we feel ourselves invigorated and refreshed.

Earth and Creation

Scientists explain the origin of our planet and the universe in terms of a massive explosion which tore through a featureless void billions of years ago. According to (other) story-tellers, however, the existence of the Earth is a consequence of actions and motivations that are often distinctly human in character.

In many mythologies, a primal goddess is the source of creation. According to the ancient Greeks the Earth Mother, Gaia, emerged from Chaos, and many centuries earlier in the Babylonian creation stories, Tiamat, the salt-water ocean, is represented as a female dragon-like monster which must be vanquished before the ordered universe can come into existence.

Creation is an immensely dramatic act: one myth might tell how the land was forced apart from the sky in a struggle between cosmic giants; another might relate how the land was dredged up from the depths of a vast ocean by a small animal. After the initial appearance of the world, the Earth's landscape is transformed by mountains, chasms and valleys in the next stage of the monumental task of creation.

Most creation stories are the prelude to the appearance of human beings, who sometimes emerge from other worlds and sometimes are fashioned by divinities from the very substance of the Earth itself.

Mist gathered in a vast wooded landscape: in prehistoric times the slow return of colour and definition to the world with every sunrise may have stimulated thoughts about creation.

Forming the Earth

The belief in a world created out of nothingness is found in many cultures. According to the Hebrew Scriptures, Yahweh simply commanded Heaven and Earth to spring into existence. For the Zuñi people of North America it was the great god Awonawilona who brooded on the heavens and made Sun and Earth out of his essence. Some creators are said to remain active in earthly affairs, while others are believed to have receded into the remote and abstract realms from which they came.

The sexual union of male and female is a metaphor for creation in many mythologies, as in the ancient Egyptian myth of the sky goddess Nut and the earth god Geb (see p.13). More commonly the Earth is female, reflecting the consonance between nature's fecundity and the fertility of women. In one version of the creation myth of the Lower Californian Luiseño people, nothing existed in the beginning except a brother and sister, one above and one below. The brother desired his sister and forced himself on her. Eventually she gave birth to a small quantity of earth and sand, the first solid ground.

The whole Earth is seen only by gods, astronauts and machines. Humanity relies on inner, visionary space to understand creation.

Creation is often expressed in terms of a powerful and universal symbol of fertility, the egg. According to a number of Chinese and Japanese accounts, the egg yolk and the albumen which surrounds it represent the Earth floating in the cosmic waters of the heavens. However, the symbolic egg can also restrain the latent energy of creation until it is ready to burst forth. The old supreme god of Tahiti, Ta'aroa, is said to have been born in this way, breaking out of his shell to begin his work. Often, creation comes about through sacrificial death. Pan Gu, the Chinese giant, exhausted after separating earth and sky, lies down and dies, and his bodily parts become the features of the landscape and the heavens.

THE BIG BANG

The Big Bang is late 20th-century science's version of the creation story. According to this theory, the universe originated in a great cosmic thermonuclear explosion which took place between 10 and 20 thousand million years ago and sent the stars and planets flying apart from each other. No one knows whether this disintegration will continue forever, or whether the universe will eventually begin to collapse back into a fiery, imploding ball.

Many peoples have seen thunder and lightning as an outburst of divine creative energy. For the Maya they were a manifestation of the creator god Huracán, whose name is the origin of the word hurricane.

CREATING THE WORLD IN SAND

In the Male Shootingway, an important curing ritual of the Navaho people of Arizona and New Mexico, the medicine man and those associated with the patient create a sacred sandpainting depicting the figures Father Sky and Mother Earth. The complex images are in effect a re-creation of the world, designed to restore the patient's physical and spiritual harmony. The traditional Navaho mud hut, the hogan, is emptied of domestic objects and the floor is prepared. The space is consecrated and the task of creating the "painting" with sand, pollens and powdered charcoal (right) begins. The images represent creators, objects

and events at the beginning of time. The place where humans are said to have emerged is symbolized by a small bowl of water buried in the sand of Mother Earth. After the sandpainting is finished, a thin line of corn pollen is run between the figures. The line represents the sacred path that is believed to be taken by all supernatural beings, and the patient's path to harmony.

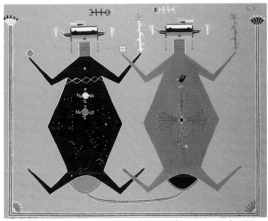

Mother Earth (left) and Father Sky, one of approximately 600 sandpainting designs used in Navaho rituals. They play a relatively brief but crucial role in curing ceremonies which may last for more than three days and nights. After use they are simply swept away.

Earth, sky and the cosmos

The skies are viewed in many traditions as a supernatural abode of divinities and cosmic forces that have a direct influence on human beings. In ancient Judaic cosmology the firmament was a solid dome pierced by windows, above which was a dome of water and, beyond that, Heaven, the dwelling place of God. The ancient Babylonians also conceived of a three-layered realm of the heavens, and other cultures describe four, seven or more levels. Parallel worlds, invisible from Earth, are often believed to exist in the skies. According to Huron and Iroquois myths, the founder of the human race was a woman, Ataentsic, who fell to Earth from the upper world through a hole in the sky. In one Navaho myth, Sky-Reaching Rock, near Mount Taylor, once grew so high that it carried the hero Younger Brother through a hole in the sky into the upper world.

For the Chinese, clouds were formed from the union of yin and yang (the two cosmic forces that interacted to make the universe) and hence symbolized peace. In many cultures the gods were depicted as pursuing loves and enmities among the clouds, and more generally the sky was thought to be the location of all things invisible or nebulous.

THE BAULE MOUSE ORACLE

The Baule people of the Ivory Coast sometimes use a "mouse oracle" to solve difficult problems. The oracle is a wooden vessel split into two sections connected by a hole: the upper part is called the sky, the lower part the earth. The vessel is a model of the cosmos, reflecting the inseparable nature of the sky and earth gods. The diviner uses a field mouse as a messenger, as the creature is believed to be close to *asye*, the Earth's sacred energy, which comes from the Earth spirit Asye. The mouse is placed in the top section of the box, whereupon it runs through the hole into the lower compartment; the diviner then arranges small bones in a pattern in the upper half, scatters rice to lure the mouse and covers the vessel. After the mouse has eaten the rice and disturbed the bones, the diviner reads the revelation contained in the new pattern formed inside the box.

In many mythologies it is said that sky and earth were joined before being forced apart. According to the ancient Egyptians, Shu, the god of air, and Tefenet, the goddess of moisture, copulated to produce the earth god Geb and the sky god Nut. These deities embraced so tightly that there was no room for anything to exist between them. Nut became pregnant, but there was no space for the children to be born, until the air god Shu separated them. Maori myth tells a similar story of the sky god Rangi and earth goddess Papa being separated by their offspring.

In several traditions the earth and sky are said to be connected by a cosmic tree with its roots in the underworld and its branches in the skies (see pp.90–91). Some cultures believed that Earth and Heaven were once joined by a rope or bridge which was severed in ancient times owing to human transgression, divine anger, or both.

The sense that human beings are subject to the powers of the heavens, the key principle of astrology, is expressed too in the early baptism rites of several societies. For example, many Africans and Native North and South Americans traditionally expose newborn children to the sun and moon.

Jacob's Dream *by William Blake (1757–1827). The idea of a ladder (or a staircase) to Heaven expresses our aspiration toward the divine.* Genesis *describes Jacob's dream of a "ladder set up on the Earth, and the top of it reaches to Heaven: and behold the angels of God ascending and descending on it". Early Christian writers treated each rung as a stage of spiritual growth.*

Races of clay

In some creation myths the first human being is said to be fashioned from the mud, sand or clay of the Earth. The Tahitian creator Ta'aroa is said to have used the earth of Tahiti to conjure up Ti'i, the first man, who appeared, appropriately for the first inhabitant of an island fringed by beaches, "clothed in sand". According to the Hopi people of North America, Spider Woman, the great weaver of the universe, spun the First People from the four colours of the earth – yellow, red, white and black – and in so doing set the pattern for this society's ritual sandpaintings (see p.11).

The Earth's raw materials do not always prove suitable for the purposes of creation. According to the 16th-century *Popol Vuh*, the great traditional history of the Quiché people of Guatemala, the grandmother of all creatures tried to create men from clay and dirt but, because they were soft and malleable and failed to make good servants, she destroyed them.

The ancient Mesopotamian goddess Mami was more successful when she mixed clay and spittle with the flesh and blood of a god to make the first seven men and seven women (as described in the story of Atrahasis, opposite). Her choice of heterogeneous materials for the sacred act of creation demonstrates the importance of bringing together physical and spiritual essence. An important tool in Mami's task was an ordinary mud brick, the use of which connected the origins of the people with the mud-brick of their dwellings, villages and temples, and in the process highlighted the sacred nature of even the most routine tasks of life.

Ancient Chinese emperors had vast, lifesize terracotta armies constructed as a sign of their power and in order to accompany and protect them in their journey through the afterlife.

THE POTTING OF HUMANKIND

The intrusion of routine labour into creation myths shows how everyday experience can inform the spiritual beliefs of a society. According to the ancient Egyptians, the ram-headed god Khnum moulded human beings on a potter's wheel. Believing that God fashions children in the womb, women of Rwanda leave water ready, before retiring to sleep, so that God may use it to form the clay of which human beings are made. In ancient Babylon the potter's craft was seen as analogous to the shaping of life, and the words for rebirth were: "We are as fresh-baked pots."

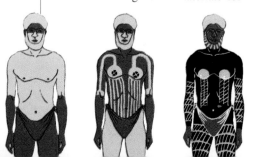

The earth provides many colourful pigments with which aboriginal Tiwi dancers of the Melville and Bathurst Islands, off the coast of Australia's Northern Territory, decorate themselves prior to an initiation ceremony.

MESOPOTAMIAN CREATION MYTH: AN EXTRACT FROM THE STORY OF ATRAHASIS

The author of this text is Nur-Aya, who inscribed it on clay tablets during the reign of Ammi-saduqa, king of Babylon (1702–1682BC).

Geshtu-e, a god who had intelligence,
They [the great gods] slaughtered in their assembly.
Nintu mixed clay
With his flesh and blood.
They heard the drumbeat forever after.
A ghost came into existence from the god's flesh,
And she [Nintu] proclaimed it as his living sign.
The ghost existed so as not to forget [the slain god].
After she had mixed that clay,
She called up the Anunnaki, the great gods.
The Igigi, the great gods,
Spat spittle upon the clay.
Mami [Nintu] made her voice heard
And spoke to the great gods,
"I have carried out perfectly
The work that you ordered of me.
You have slaughtered a god together with his intelligence.
I have relieved you of your hard work,
I have imposed your load on man,
You have bestowed noise on mankind.
I have undone the fetter and granted freedom."
They listened to this speech of hers,
And were freed [from anxiety], and kissed her feet:
"We used to call you Mami
But now your name shall be Mistress of All Gods."
Far-sighted Enki and wise Mami
Went into the room of fate.
The womb-goddesses were assembled.
He trod the clay in her presence;
She kept reciting an incantation,
For Enki, staying in her presence, made her recite it.
When she finished her incantation,
She pinched off fourteen pieces [of clay],
[And set] seven pieces on the right,
Seven on the left.
Between them she put down a mud brick.
She made use of [?] a reed, opened it [?] to cut the umbilical cord,
Called up the wise and knowledgeable
Womb-goddesses, seven and seven.
Seven created males,
Seven created females,
For the womb-goddess [is] creator of fate.

Source: Tablet 1 of *Atrahasis*, translated by Stephanie Dalley in *Myths from Mesopotamia*, Stephanie Dalley, Oxford University Press, 1989, pp.15–17. Quoted by permission.

The Ancient Mother

The belief that the traditional notion of "mother nature" is rooted in a long-forgotten prehistoric religion devoted to the worship of an all-powerful Earth goddess (the Ancient Mother or Great Mother) has many adherents in the West today.

The concept appeals to feminists for its anti-patriarchal implications and to ecologists for its suggestion of due respect awarded to nature.

Some scholars have suggested that the first perceived deity was indeed a goddess who created the world from herself; that early religions were dominated by worship of this supreme being; and, by extension, that early societies were matriarchal. This hypothesis is based mainly on the evidence of prehistoric cave paintings, carvings and pottery remains. The carvings, such as the so-called "Venus" discovered at Laussel in the Dordogne, France, and the numerous other "Venus" figurines (see opposite),

The exaggerated thighs of this 6,000-year-old figure from Anatolia suggest that she may have been associated with fertility rituals.

strongly suggest that the association between women and fertility was acknowledged and even celebrated in Paleolithic times. However, they do not prove the existence of an early belief system focused on the worship of an Earth mother, and any attempt to go even further and extrapolate, as some have done, a matriarchal model for the most ancient societies is at best pure speculation.

As more settled agricultural societies developed during the later Neolithic age, spiritual concerns evidently came to focus more upon the fertility of the Earth. In the 1960s, during archaeological excavations at the ancient Anatolian town of Çatal Hüyük, which flourished c.6500–c.5700BC, an enthroned female figure apparently giving birth and flanked by leopards was found in a grain bin next to a shrine. Some experts saw the figure as evidence of a religion based upon the Ancient Mother, but others insisted that it represented only a minor fertility goddess. The figure rests her hands, with apparent affection, on the leopards' heads, leading some to interpret her as a Mistress of Animals.

During the Bronze Age, at the time of the Minoan civilization centred on Crete (c.1400–c.1100BC), palace shrines were built at Knossos, Gournia, Phaistos and Mallia. Each was set in a similar landscape and appears to form part of a vast female figure: the palaces are close to a pair of mountains resembling breasts and beneath a rounded hill that may represent a woman's belly. These settings are not proof that the Minoans worshipped a supreme goddess, but do suggest that they recognized a sacred, female power within the living world.

Earthwoman, a grass-topped figure nearly 30 feet(10m) long, created in 1976–7 by James Pierce on a farm in Maine, reflects the fascination with a primal mother goddess.

VENUS FIGURINES

The female statuettes known as Venus figurines appeared across Europe during the Upper Paleolithic era (*c.*35,000–*c.*10,000BC). Carved from stone, bone and ivory and shaped from clay, many examples, such as the Venus of Willendorf, are naked, fleshy females with large pendulous breasts, big buttocks and swollen bellies. This physique suggests an association with fertility. Moreover, the statues have no feet: the legs taper to a point, suggesting that they could be stuck upright in soft earth and worshipped. Some experts have argued that the women's unwieldy shape is intended subliminally to suggest that they would be more comfortable sitting or lying down – thereby becoming joined to the body of Earth.

Rather than goddesses, Venus figurines may have been emblems of social identity used to cement social relationships among widely dispersed groups of mobile hunters at the end of the Paleolithic era. It is also possible that some of the figurines may be portraits of actual women. Certainly, archaeologists have discovered hundreds of stone slabs inscribed with drawings that date from the same era as the Venus figurines, and among them are some striking and highly individual representations.

The limestone Venus of Willendorf, from Austria, is at least 25,000 years old. Its height is just over 4 inches (10cm).

The goddess of the West

Several female deities of the ancient Mediterranean world have been interpreted as embodiments of the idea of the "Ancient Mother". For example, the Greek goddesses Gaia, Rhea, Demeter and Hera all shared the attributes of nurturing and fertility and were associated, more generally, with nature. Cybele, a great Earth and mother goddess who originated in Phrygia in central Asia Minor (present-day Turkey), probably came closest to the concept of a supreme Earth goddess. She was referred to by the Romans as Magna Mater (Great Mother), and her influence was such that in 204BC, at the behest of the Delphic oracle, her statue was brought by boat from Pergamum in Asia Minor to Rome in the belief that it would aid the Romans in their war against the Carthaginians. Rome was ambivalent about this goddess: on the one hand, her ecstatic cult with its self-castrated priests and wild revelry

seemed alien in character; on the other hand, because her homeland, near Troy, was taken as the cradle of the Roman race, she was treated as a "native" deity.

With the spread of Christianity, public worship increasingly centred on a male supreme deity. However, Mother Earth was kept alive outside the Church by popular religion and by folk beliefs about the natural world. Well into the Christian era, Cybele continued to be worshipped under the name of Berecynthia: as late as the 6th century AD, Gregory of Tours watched as Gallo-Roman peasants drove a statue of Cybele around their fields in the hope that the goddess might protect their crops. And at Eleusis in Attica, Greek peasants continued to worship Demeter into modern times, referring to her as Mistress of the Earth and Sea.

In AD431 the Virgin Mary was officially declared Mother of God, thereby inheriting the title of Cybele, known to the Greeks as Meter Theon, Mother of the Gods. The council at which Mary's

The Virgin Mary is borne through Guatemala City on Good Friday. The leaves and flowers in her carriage may be a relic of fertility rituals.

The Earth goddess Demeter with the gods Hermes, Ares and Dionysos, on the east frieze of the Parthenon, Athens (447–438BC).

status was proclaimed was held at Ephesus, an ancient Greek centre of goddess worship. The cult of the Blessed Virgin Mary quickly spread throughout the Christian world and flourishes to this day. Mary took on many attributes of pre-Christian goddesses, and several of her shrines were formerly consecrated to female deities. For example, the 4th-century patriarch of Constantinople, Epiphanus, saw Arabian women making offerings to the Virgin at a shrine where their ancestors had once worshipped the Near Eastern goddess Ashtoreth. In Mexico the Virgin of Guadalupe was accepted as the country's national symbol by the indigenous people because they regarded her as an incarnation of Tonantsi, the Aztec Earth and mother goddess.

THE CULT OF ST BRIDE

In the 9th century an Irish king-bishop compiled a glossary in which he listed an ancient goddess, Brighid. Little is known of this deity, but it seems that she may have been an Earth goddess. There were sometimes said to be three Brighids, each representing a particular aspect of the deity, which links her to the mother goddess triads of Celtic Britain and Gaul.

With the arrival of Christianity in the 5th century, the Irish began to revere a saint who bore the goddess's name (she was known as Bride or Bridget) and shared her feast day of February 1, the pagan festival of Imbolc, associated with the

Minerva and the Muses, by Hans Jordaens (1595–1644). The Romano-Celtic goddess Minerva is identified with Brighid.

lactation of ewes. The saint inherited other aspects of the goddess: her cows were said to yield a lake of milk, her food supply was endless, and one measure of her malt could make enough ale to go round among all her churches. In popular belief St Bride presides over the domestic hearth and childbirth and protects flocks. She is also the foster-mother of Christ.

Woman as the Goddess

This 11th-century manuscript shows the goddess of the Earth as Nature herself arising from the ground.

A romantic, soft-focused notion of the Mother Earth was used in the 19th century to shore up the widespread cult of idealized femininity. An ironic parallel to this is the strategy in modern times whereby women across the Western world have been turning to ancient Earth goddesses as a means of legitimizing female power. They have looked for inspiration to goddesses such as Cybele, Rome's Magna Mater, who can be terrifying and chaotic as well as nurturing, and Kali, the Hindu goddess, who is both fearsome and benevolent.

For many women, the great Earth goddesses offer liberation precisely because they contain all aspects and all contradictions, just as nature itself is both creator and destroyer. Christianity, by contrast, is sometimes viewed as having polarized cultural notions of femininity into the earthly, carnal temptress Eve and the irreproachable Virgin Mary, for whom birth is a process outside nature.

In many tribal societies the Earth goddess embodies birth, death and rebirth – the endless cycle to which humankind must learn to be reconciled. The Earth goddess does not try to deny death by promising eternal life, but instead celebrates death as a part of the rhythm of nature.

The Ibo of Nigeria often portray Mother Earth holding a large knife, because she symbolizes both abundant vitality and its opposite; and in a myth of the North American Huron people, the goddess Yatahéntshi was both the mother of humanity and the keeper of the dead.

In the ancient Anatolian town of Çatal Hüyük (*c.*6500–*c.*5700BC) several buildings have shrines with breast-like objects protruding from their walls. These strange, suggestive shapes have been moulded around the skulls of vultures, foxes and weasels, their sharp beaks and teeth forming the nipples. All these creatures are scavengers. It would seem that the people of Çatal Hüyük made a spiritual association between women and death.

The intense interest shown in the ancient Earth goddesses in modern times reflects a view of the world made up, not of warring opposites, but of continually unfolding processes. The sacred is widely seen as being somehow

An advert for an ideal kitchen of the 1950s shows woman typecast as provider (ice in this case is her special element). The image is vibrant with feminist issues and contradictions.

inherent in nature, rather than transcending nature. Undoubtedly, as with many philosophical issues, the reliance upon intuitive logic ensures that the debate will thrive.

SERPENT GODDESSES

In the Neolithic era, Earth goddesses were often represented bearing aloft snakes, ancient symbols of healing and fertility. However, when male-dominated pantheons began to encroach on Earth-centred beliefs, the serpent goddesses were dethroned.

The oracle at Delphi, identified with the Earth goddess Gaia, was looked after by a priestess called the Pythia, who received the oracles while seated on a

A Persian snake goddess.

tripod around which a snake called Python entwined itself. After a tremendous battle, Apollo was said to have killed Python and taken over the shrine. Thus, a sky god who was linked with sickness (but also, to complicate matters, healing) vanquished the embodiment of healing and fruitfulness.

Where dragons and serpents appear in myths (such as the Babylonian creation myth: see p.8), it is possible that they are a subliminal allegory signifying the old matriarchal religion.

The body of the Earth

The belief in the living essence of our planet gains concrete and powerful expression when specific landscape features are interpreted as forming part of the body of a great supernatural being.

To the Thompson people of British Columbia, Earth-woman was long ago transformed into the present world: her hair became the trees and grass, her flesh became the earth, her bones became the rocks, her blood became the waters. The Babylonian epic of creation tells how the god Marduk killed Tiamat, the goddess of watery chaos. He sliced her in two "like a fish for drying", then forced one half up into an arch to form the roof of the sky, heaped the lower half with mountains; then he pierced it to form water courses. In Norse mythology, the primeval giant Ymir rose out of the union of ice and fire and created earth from his body, the seas from his blood and the heavens from his skull.

Cultures that view the Earth as a parent not surprisingly believe that it can provide direct physical nourishment. According to the Aztec Legend of the Sun, the original Mexica people were born in a cave and were suckled by the spirit of the Earth, Mecitli. In ancient Egyptian myth the Earth and mother goddess Hathor was pictured as a cow, the provider of life-giving milk.

Caves and holes in the ground are in many regions viewed as vaginas, wombs or other openings into Mother Earth (or sometimes exits from the underworld). The shrine of Kamakhya Devi in eastern India is a natural rock cleft which Hindus traditionally believe to be the vagina of the goddess who is said to menstruate once a year during a festival held in her honour. This direct cor-

This early 20th-century photograph shows a group of girls dancing around a phallic menhir in Brittany, France, in the hope of ensuring future fertility.

A rock crevice pictured as part of a female figure at a prehistoric site in Canada.

respondence between the natural landscape and the deities whose physical presence is believed to reside in that landscape is also found in rock art where, for example, a painter or carver has seen a natural crevice as a vulva and incorporated it into a picture.

Stone monoliths in many cultures are regarded as phallic. In rural Brittany childless women made pilgrimages to ancient stone menhirs, seeing them as concentrations of male sexual potency: by offering up prayers to the stones they believed they would become more fertile. In India the god Shiva is represented by a phallic pillar known as a lingam – one of many associations between divinity and virility.

It is believed by many New Agers that the "male" and "female" stones of Men-an-Tol, near Morvah in Cornwall, southwestern England, channel earth energy, giving them healing power.

THE SIPAPU

According to the creation myth of the Hopi people of North America, human beings entered the present world at an opening called the *sipapu*. This drama of emergence is re-enacted during the *wuwuchim* ceremony, a celebration of rebirth. The rite is held in secret once every four years in a dome-shaped sacred structure known as the *kiva*. The *kiva* is conceived of as Mother Earth herself. A small hole in the centre of the floor represents the *sipapu* and a ladder through a hole in the roof is seen as the umbilical cord leading out to the next world. During the ritual, initiates make the transition to adulthood.

THE MERCIFUL PHALLUS

In the city of Petra, Jordan, the capital of the ancient Nabataean kingdom that flourished c.150BC–c.AD150, two obelisks stand on the summit of a sandstone mountain (right). The Nabataeans were an Arabian people who lived between what are now Syria and Saudi Arabia. They carved the mountain away to leave the

The twin pillars of Zibb Attuf.

pillars, which stand about 20 feet (6m) high and 100 feet (30m) apart. The landmarks appear to have a religious purpose and may represent the male and female divinities Dusares and Al Uzza. Almost certainly, they were symbols of fertility, and the site is known to modern Bedouin Arabs as Zibb Attuf, "The Place of the Merciful Phallus", suggesting a continuing tradition of sexual associations.

The world's navel

The most sacred stone of ancient Greece once stood in the oracle chamber of Apollo's shrine at Delphi, on the southern slope of Mount Parnassus. According to the Greek poet Hesiod, writing in the 8th century BC, the egg-shaped stone had been placed there by Zeus and stood next to the tripod on which the priestess sat to deliver her prophesies, possibly inspired by narcotic vapours emanating from the depths of the Earth. The Greeks regarded this stone as the centre of the world and called it the *omphalos*, or navel; in doing so, they symbolically connected the stone with the body of the goddess Gaia, who was seen as the Earth itself.

The omphalos *at Delphi, where the priestess of Apollo gave her prophecies.*

Another *omphalos* was located on the island of Crete, a sacred place where the umbilical cord of Zeus was believed to have fallen to the Earth after his birth. The sites of these two navel stones, at Delphi and on Crete, symbolically brought together the supreme god Zeus and the Earth goddess Gaia, and were seen as the dual source of all the world's creative energy, the wellspring of life itself.

In some cultures, the navel is believed to be manifested in natural features of the Earth. Sometimes weathered mountains, their peaks reaching up to the heavens, are said to mark the cosmic centre. Mount Gerizim in Palestine was described in the Hebrew Scriptures (Old Testament) as the navel of the Earth, and the name of Mount Tabor derives from the Hebrew word for navel, *tabur*. The rock on which Jerusalem was built was also seen as a kind of navel: according to Hebrew tradition it was the spiritual centre of the holy lands, the pivot of creation; it is also sacred to Muslims as the place where Muhammad ascended into Heaven.

The cosmic centre, which may also be marked by a tree, pillar or other symbolic focus, provides a reassurance, in the landscape, of a world in which harmony and order have positive meaning.

The prominent dome of Mount Tabor, the traditional site of Christ's transfiguration, is seen as a centre of spiritual energy.

There are potentially as many symbolic world centres as there are social groups. The Pueblo Indian Tewa people, for example, see every village as a microcosm of the world, framed at the cardinal points by four sacred mountains, four sacred hills, four shrines, four dance plazas within the village and, at the centre, the most sacred spot, known as "earth mother earth navel middle place".

The Dome of the Rock in Jerusalem (above), revered by Muslims as the navel of the world.

The decorated passage at Gavrinis tomb, Brittany.

THE JOURNEY TO THE CENTRE OF THE EARTH

The stories of the French writer Jules Verne (1828–1905), who is often regarded as the father of modern science fiction, tended to be based on scientific theories, inventions and accounts by travellers, and show his fascination with themes of geographical space and territory. The *omphalos* or central point is a recurrent motif. Verne's perhaps most successful work, *A Journey to the Centre of the Earth* (first published in 1864), is a geological epic in which, typically for Verne, prosaic science and poetic fantasy are skilfully combined to produce a compelling account that inverts the more commonplace fascination of adventures in outer space. One influence on the novel was the theory posited by John Cleves Synmes, of the US Infantry, that the Earth was hollow and made up of five concentric spheres, with openings several thousands of miles wide at the poles. Interwoven with this idea was the theory expounded by Charles Sainte-Claire Deville, a distinguished French geographer who was also a friend of Verne's, that all the volcanoes of Europe were interconnected by a network of subterranean passages.

MEGALITHIC NAVELS

Many megalithic monuments in Europe make explicit reference to male and female anatomy in their construction and decoration. At the passage grave of Gavrinis, on a small island in the Gulf of Morbihan in Brittany, 23 upright stone slabs which line the passages are completely incised with complex abstract designs. Each design is a set of increasingly larger arcs which extend outwards from a vulvic shape in the centre. Some researchers have interpreted this pattern as a belly with an *omphalos* protruding at the top, executed in an attempt to connect the dead with the navel of the Earth.

The domed mound of Silbury Hill in Wiltshire, England (see pp.106–107), might also be said to resemble the belly of a goddess: the *omphalos* is the circular summit of the hill.

Mankind and the elements

Many civilizations have viewed man as a microcosm of the universe. In the principal stream of thought, which informed the alchemical tradition of Europe, four primal elements (Earth, Air, Fire and Water) combined and interacted to produce every phenomenon in nature. In the human body they were represented by four fluids or humours (see opposite, below).

According to Mithraism, a mystery cult of Persian origin that was popular in the Roman Empire, man had to rule the elements before he could attain spiritual wisdom. An initiate into the cult had to undergo rites of Earth, Air, Water and Fire, each of which tested a different aspect of his nature. Hermeticism, which is based on 42 books of mystic wisdom dating from the 3rd century BC to the 1st century AD, and attributed to a divine master of magic lore known as Hermes Tris-

An early 19th-century Indian painting showing the god Vishnu represented as the whole world.

In this Chinese woodcut (left) the human body is represented as a mountain.

megistus ("Thrice-Great Hermes"), centred on the belief that in order to attain perfection, man must reflect rather than rule the elements. According to the Hermetic *Emerald Tablet*: "That which is above is like that which is below and that which is below is like that which is above, to achieve the wonders of the one thing." This principle formed the basis of alchemy: man was the image of god and contained the essence, the *prima materia*, of the universe. Humanity was therefore linked spiritually and physically both to the living nature and to the heavens – the source of wisdom and understanding.

Chinese myth tells how the ordered world sprang from the cosmic giant Pan Gu: his tears made the rivers, his breath the wind, his voice thunder, the flashing

A 15th-century French image showing man as a microcosm of the heavens: each sign of the zodiac corresponds to a region of the body.

of his eyes lightning. His eyes became the sun and moon and other parts of his body formed five sacred mountains.

Elemental thinking also characterizes the symbolism of the heart. In the *Vedas*, the early sacred texts of India, the heart is organized in symbols: in its "lotus flower" is a small place containing heaven, earth, sun, moon and stars. In Taoism the heart is sited between Heaven (head) and Earth (abdomen), and its transmutation to a chamber of fire will make its owner immortal.

An idea central to the Chinese tradition is a fivefold division of the universe into the Taoist elements: Water, Fire, Wood, Metal and Earth. A similar system was followed in India, where the elements of Akasha (ether), Apas (water), Vayu (air), Tejas (fire) and Privithi (earth) were seen as "cosmic states of vibration".

THE ELEMENTS AND THE TEMPERAMENTS

In the human body the elements were traditionally represented by the four fluids or humours: Melancholia or Black Bile (Earth); Blood (Air); Choler (Fire); Phlegm (Water). Various physical and spiritual attributes were ascribed to each element or humour, and the predominance of one or other determined the character of the person or thing. In general, Earth and Water represented the female principle and Air and Fire the male principle. Earth also represented stability, darkness and the materialization of cosmic powers: a

person in whom its equivalent humour, Melancholia, was dominant was said to have a "melancholic" temperament. In a similar way, people were

A 16th-century print showing the elements related to the four temperaments.

described as "sanguine" (from *sanguis*, the Latin for "blood"), "choleric" or else "phlegmatic" depending on their prevailing humour.

In Western alchemy the four elements were surrounded by a purer fifth essence, the Quintessence, which was believed by Aristotle to be distinct from the others. There are analogies here with *prana*, the Eastern notion of an energizing etheric spirit.

Alchemy often uses animal symbols, such as the eagle (air), the phoenix (fire), the dolphin (water). The lion and snake are both symbols of raw, unrefined matter: sometimes the lion is shown eating the sun (the male principle).

Gaia returns

It is often argued today that the submergence of the "female" values of nature, sympathy and intuition has brought with it a profound and very dangerous d e t a c h m e n t from the natural world. This trend may be traced in the history of science, and particularly in the development in the 17th century of a mechanistic view of the universe. The influence of the scientific revolution is still prevalent, and many claim that it has led the West to inflict damage on the Earth by encouraging people to view nature as inanimate matter, robust in its weathering of pollution and other environmental harm. However, in the latter half of the 20th century a holistic approach to nature has arisen which treats the Earth as a developing organism whose parts relate to one another in a complex balance, just as our cells, organs, nervous system and other bodily (and less determinable) components together make up a human being.

In the 1970s the British biochemist James E. Lovelock put forward the

According to the Italian poet Boccaccio (1313–75), Gaia Cyrilla, shown here, ignored her noble and womanly upbringing and took up weaving. Like her namesake the Greek goddess, this heroine embodies qualities long perceived in Western culture as female.

Gaia hypothesis (named after the Greek Earth goddess) that the Earth is a self-regulating, living organism, which reacts to threats posed to it in such a way as to maximize its own chances for survival. Lovelock published his theories in 1979 in his highly influential book, *Gaia: A New Look at Life on Earth*. He argues that living things and the e n v i r o n m e n t evolve together in a complementary way, to create a delicately poised system. The balance between atmospheric carbon dioxide and oxygen maintained by living organisms creates conditions in which life forms thrive. Lovelock explains how the salt concentration in the world's oceans has remained constant at approximately 3.5 per cent ever since the oceans first came into existence: the salt added to the seas always equals the amount removed (for example, through the drying up of lagoons), and only this constant balance makes marine life possible.

An understanding of this vast natural machinery makes us aware both of the insignificance of human beings in planetary terms and of the very high costs that we will have to pay if we abuse our power to change the environment. To paraphrase Lovelock, Gaia has both her benevolent and harsh aspects, making the world comfortable for those who follow the rules, but punishing transgressors ruthlessly. The idea that the survival of humankind depends on an organism greater than ourselves, which would sacrifice our species to keep itself alive, has become one of the central planks of the Green movement.

Many people see a close affinity between the Gaia hypothesis and the manner in which tribal peoples view the Earth and their relation to it. As one Native American leader, Chief Seattle, expressed it in the mid-19th century: "The Earth does not belong to man, man belongs to the Earth. ... Man did not weave the web of life, he is merely a strand in it. Whatever he does to the web, he does to himself."

THE NEW AGE OF GAIA

Followers of the New Age movement support the holistic implications of the Gaia hypothesis. They believe that all life is interrelated and that the only way forward for humanity is through a balanced coexistence with the environment. Many proponents of this idea see Native North America as an inspiring example of a culture in which the connection between Earth and people is both balanced

and profound. There is an element of romanticization here, which has led some Westerners to appropriate

A sun dance ritual of the Sioux, drawn by Short Bull, 1912.

Native American ritual as a vehicle for drawing closer to Gaia, the natural world.

Other New Agers have sought inspiration from the Gaea hypothesis developed in California by Otter Zell. According to Zell, Gaea (this is the latinized spelling of Gaia) is the archetypal mother goddess. In 1970 Zell founded a movement devoted to her, after having a vision in which he saw the Earth as one vast living organism which had evolved from a single original cell.

Increasing numbers of Westerners, disillusioned with materialism, are turning to Native American culture in an attempt to bring about a "re-connection" with nature.

Spirit Paths and Landscapes

The history of the Earth, whether told by scientists or by shamans, is a tale of tumultuous change – one that has left its mark on the planet's surface.

Many cultures have believed that in the distant past supernatural beings roamed the world, transforming it as they went. These beings wrought lakes, mountains, rock outcrops and seas, either intentionally or unwittingly, and their dwellings and resting places, it is thought, may still be seen. Supposed traces of mythic human ancestors and heroes are similarly resonant, with a symbolism that can be important to a culture's (or a nation's) sense of identity.

For societies that possess a profound sense of the sacred, no terrain can be merely geophysical: there is always some inherent, animated meaning. The chapter that follows explores various manifestations, in a range of cultures, of sacred vitality in the landscape around us.

The formation of landscape features, such as this dramatically contoured gully in the Arizona desert, has been attributed in many cultures to the actions of supernatural beings, often perceived as giants. Even in Europe, where myths of the landscape are not a major strand in the surviving tradition, many place-names refer to folkloric associations between prominent geological landmarks and mythical figures such as King Arthur and Finn mac Cumhaill.

Mental maps

A person's view of the physical landcape is determined by individual experience, cultural background, and spiritual outlook. In the early Judaic and Christian traditions, worldviews have been based on the Hebrew Scripture. One drawing of the 6th century AD represented the Earth as a rectangular box, the tabernacle of Moses: within the

Formal gardens, such as this 19th-century Italian design, echoed ideas of a perfect, ordered nature found in the ancient Persian pairidaeza ("walled garden") – whence the word "paradise".

tal lines marked by sacred monuments. Delphi represented, likewise, the sacred heart of the Greek cosmos: it was the navel of the Earth (see pp.24–5), which itself was envisaged as the body of a goddess, Gaia. Until the 17th century in the West the Earth itself was seen as the focal point of God's creation.

Just as the Earth's shape and location are viewed in a variety of ways, so an individual environment may be endowed with varying degrees of spiritual significance to create what has been termed a mythologized landscape. In many cultures features of the landscape may be significant elements in a sacred repository of spiritual knowledge and ancestral wisdom which is often crucial to survival. For example, the Pawnee people of the North American plains once hunted within a territory that was denoted by five important sacred sites, where the

Nahalal, a modern Israeli settlement. Urban planning often satisfies a profound need for symmetry.

box was a mountain, the Earth, surrounded by ocean, and the lid of the box was the sky. Other medieval maps showed the holy city of Jerusalem, the spiritual centre of the world, as its physical centre also. Cosmological focal points reflect a culture's sense of identity. The Inca empire was seen spiritually as a series of lines radiating from the capital, Cuzco, the course of these men-

game animals were believed to assemble. As long as the Pawnee hunters remained within the landscape demarcated by these sites and made offerings at them, they maintained their close spiritual relationship with the creatures whose meat and hide they were dependent upon. The oceanic environment of the Polynesians is traditionally viewed in a similar way: for them, maritime lore is not simply awareness of observable phenomena gained by experience, but sacred wisdom from the gods bestowed on the navigators to whom it was essential for survival.

The Maori of New Zealand are among the numerous peoples who recognize specific parts of the landscape – fishing grounds, rocks, trees, rivers, caves and ridges – as places which their ancestors visited and named. These natural features communicate ancient knowledge and history to any Maori who passes by. A similar view of the landscape prevails among Aboriginal Australians and the peoples of Papua New Guinea.

Many oral traditions convey sacred and practical ideas about the environment simultaneously. For example, an Alaskan Nunamiut boy must learn about his local terrain in great detail before taking his place in the hunt. Topographical information is conveyed to him in myths of the spirits, tricksters and heroes who are said to have populated the hunting grounds. Through the mythic drama he builds up a symbolic picture of his surroundings to guide him when he takes to the trails himself.

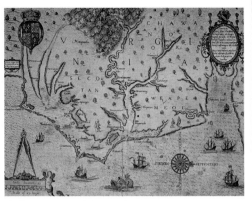

An English map of Virginia (1585). European cartographers viewed the Native American sacred landscape in terms of their own assumptions. Western mapmaking is no more objective in essence than more obviously belief-inspired representations.

TROPHY ARRAYS

The Wopkaimin people of Mountain Ok in central New Guinea display game animal bones and other trophies on the walls of their houses in such a way that they map the position of the animals or trophies both in the natural and social environments. Ancestral relics and the mandibles of sacrificial pigs come from the village area, and are placed in the centre of the display; the relics, the most important objects, are placed at eye level and the pig bones just below. Wild pig bones come from the bottom zone of the rainforest, and are placed at the bottom of the display. Marsupials live in the upper zone, and their bones are at the top. The bones of cassowaries, birds found in both zones, are distributed in both the upper and lower parts of the display.

As the array builds up, it becomes a symbolic map of the landscape in which the Wopkaimin live and hunt, reflecting the numbers and habitat of the animals hunted. By studying the array, the Wopkaimin can gain a graphic impression of their environment, information which will help them to plan their future hunting strategies.

This Japanese Zen garden reflects the uncluttered inner peace which is a goal of Zen Buddhism.

Songlines

According to the traditional belief of Aboriginal Australians, all things began with the Dreaming (also called the Dreamtime or Creation Period), an epoch when ancestral creator spirit beings lived on Earth. These spirits, which are said to have taken the forms of people, animals, plants or inanimate objects, could change shape at will and their existence is revealed by the marks they left on the landscape.

The Aboriginals believe that the Dreaming spirits, as they travelled across the Earth, created and named animals, rocks, trees, waterholes and other natural features. They also deposited the spirits of unborn children and determined the forms of human society. A group of sites is often associated with a particular ancestral spirit as landmarks denoting the course of its travels. The routes of these spirit ancestors are called Dreaming tracks or "songlines". At each site the spirit is believed to have left either spiritual essence or physical remains such as footprints, body impressions or dung. For example, the Yarralin people of the

Near Alice Springs, an Aranda elder explains the sacred Yippirringa Dreaming rock paintings.

Victoria River valley in Northern Territory regard the spirit Walujapi as the Dreaming ancestor of the black-headed python. Walujapi left a snake-like track along a cliff face and the imprint of her buttocks when she sat down to camp. Both features are visible today.

The Australian landscape is criss-crossed with songlines, some of which are no more than a few miles long, while others extend for hundreds of miles through various types of terrain and pass through the lands of many different Aboriginal groups, who may speak different languages and subscribe to different traditions. For example, the Native Cat Dreaming ancestors are said to have begun their journey at the sea and to have moved north into the

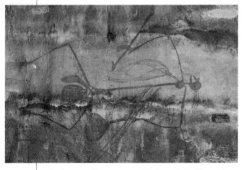

An image of an ancestral being of the Dreaming called Lightning Man, painted on Obiri Rock near Katherine, Northern Territory.

Simpson Desert, traversing as they did so the lands of the Aranda, Unmatjera, Kaititja, Ilpara, Ngalia and Kukatja. Each Aboriginal group tells that part of the myth which relates to events that took place in its territory.

Among the Yarralin people, the Pigeon Dreaming story tells how two pigeons, a brother and sister, followed the Victoria River from the edge of the desert to the coastal region. On the first leg of their journey they spoke the Gurindji language but each time they crossed into a different Aboriginal country they adopted the language of the people who would live there. This songline, like many others, provides common ground among culturally disparate Aboriginal groups.

At the end of the Dreaming the spirit beings either became the species they represented or retreated into the earth. The landscape remained as they created it, and their dwelling places and the sites of important Dreaming events are seen as sources of great power. Aboriginals believe that the spiritual seed of every individual derives from a specific site created by beings of the Dreaming. Consequently, each person's identity is intimately tied to the landscape.

THE LIVING DREAMING

When the Dreaming ended, all things were fixed – the forms of the landscape and its life, the organization of societies and the guardianship of land. However, the Dreaming continues to play an important role in Aboriginal life. For example, anyone born near a sacred Dreaming site is seen as the incarnation of its associated being, and becomes the site's guardian. Aboriginal holy men, known as *karadjis* or "men of high degree", are believed to be in direct contact with the Dreaming and its spirit beings. They sometimes wear feathers on their ankles to symbolize their ability to "fly" to the spirit realms, and are the only people who may create new dances, songs and stories about the Dreaming.

An anthropologist studying the Pintupi of the Western Desert recently witnessed the discovery by a group of men of an unusual multicoloured sedimentary rock on the bank of a creek. Elders were summoned to interpret the find, and one claimed that it was related to the Kangaroo Dreaming, in which two ancestral heroes speared a kangaroo several miles from the creek. The elders agreed that the wounded kangaroo must have crawled along the creek to try to reach his own country, but the heroes caught up with him and gutted his carcass on this spot. The rock, therefore, was the entrails of the kangaroo.

Toby, an Aboriginal elder, celebrates the exploits of his sacred Dreaming ancestors by drawing a symbolic songline in the sand at Uluru (Ayers Rock: see p.64) to accompany his telling of their story.

Sacred journeys

*God hands down the Law to Moses and the Israelites on Mount Sinai,
by John Martin (1789–1854). The Exodus represents a people's journey from servitude
to spiritual redemption in the Promised Land.*

The movement of peoples across the Earth plays a large part in the history of the human race, and it is unsurprising that great journeys of migration, exploration and conquest appear so often in myths and legends. Such journeys, many of them probably rooted in real wanderings of the distant past, may serve to explain and to justify the occupation of a land by people who still possess the sense that they were originally strangers. The migrations are often said to have been at the instigation of a divine or supernatural figure who guided and sustained the people and instructed them where to settle. This is the case with the story of the Exodus in the Hebrew Scriptures: Moses led the Israelites from servitude into a land expressly promised to them as a homeland by Yahweh.

The Exodus represented a process of communal spiritual renewal which laid the moral and religious foundations of a settled society. The same can also be said of the Aztec migration story, which is recorded in a variety of 16th-century images and texts. Probably based on a historical migration of the Aztecs from northwest Mexico that took place *c*.AD1150–1350, the tale tells of the journey of the Mexica people from the island of Aztlan to the site of their future capital city, Tenochtitlan, in the Valley of Mexico. Along the way, the Mexica gained knowledge and experience which would help them in their future homeland.

The Mexica are guided by their supreme god, Huitzilopochtli, and at the first place at which they break their journey they build a temple in his honour and receive his instructions. During their next pause, at the birthplace of the god, they are taught how to conduct a sacred fire ceremony. As the journey progresses the Mexica acquire more of the sacred rituals, skills and other cul-

TRAVELS OF THE HOPI

According to the origin myth of the Hopi people of Arizona, their ancestors rose through three lower worlds before emerging into this, the Fourth World. When they emerged, their guardian spirit told them that they had to walk to the four ends of the Earth and return before they could settle in the centre, their homeland. Each of the four clans into which the ancestors were divided was given a sacred tablet to guide it on its way. The four clans walked all over what is now North and South America, and their passing is marked to this day by ancient monuments and ruins. When members of the Snake Clan stopped in the Great Plains of North America they decided to leave a mark. Because there were no rocks on which to carve their clan symbol, they built a large earthen mound in the shape of a snake. Some Hopi today believe that the great Serpent Mound in Ohio (see pp.110–11) is the legendary mound of the Snake Clan.

Hopi dance rituals celebrate mythic ancestral journeys.

tural characteristics that distinguish them from other peoples: they learn how to control water resources when they build a dam across a river at Tula, and before reaching their destination they learn the arts of politics and warfare. They also change their name from Mexica to Aztec ("People of Aztlan"), emphasizing the extent to which the migration represents a new beginning.

The sacred wandering need not be undertaken by the people themselves in order for them to acquire its spiritual benefits. According to the Midéwiwin or Grand Medicine Society, a shamanic organization of the Ojibwa people who live around Lake Superior in North America, the spirit-being Bear brought the Ojibwa their curing rites to grant them health and long life. The Earth Spirit Shell and the Great Spirit in the sky ordered Bear to carry the sacred objects needed for the rites up through several layers of earth to the surface of the water (Lake Superior) and then through the lakes and rivers of Ojibwa territory toward Leech Lake in Minnesota. As Bear headed for the west end of Lake Superior he halted at several places to establish a Midéwiwin lodge attended by a guardian spirit. The sacred route leading from Lake Superior to Leech Lake and beyond is recorded in maps on scrolls of birchbark which are used by a Midéwiwin shaman during a curing ritual to illustrate his narrative of the sacred journey.

The Christian crusades of the Middle Ages were motivated by the belief that to conduct the Holy War in a distant land was not only justified, but pleasing to God.

Wanderings of the heroes

The heroic journey across an unknown landscape is encountered in a great number of myths and legends worldwide, from the Japanese epics of the heroes Jimmu-tenno and Yamato-takeru to the Graeco-Roman stories of Odysseus, Jason and Aeneas. The journey usually involves an individual (often of princely status and accompanied by a band of followers) who ventures from the familiar home environment into the outside world, where he (or, less frequently, she) accomplishes great deeds and overcomes many difficulties before returning home to general acclaim. For example, Homer's epic poem the *Odyssey* (*c*.750BC) relates the journey of the hero-king Odysseus from the Trojan War to his homeland of Ithaca. On the ten-year voyage he encounters many fabulous lands and monsters, but all his comrades perish.

The heroic journey has been interpreted as a metaphor for the process of individual spiritual development, wherein the varied landscapes traversed by the heroic figure stand for different aspects of the human psyche, and physical trials represent tests of spiritual endeavour. The symbolism becomes more profound if the journey takes the form of a quest. The object of the quest is generally something extremely precious that may be said to represent the goal of spiritual enlightenment or self-knowledge. In the West, the most famous example of the heroic journey as spiritual quest is the search for the Grail (see opposite, below).

The labyrinth or maze that a hero or heroine must sometimes penetrate (especially the original Labyrinth on Crete in the Greek myth of the hero Theseus) is a highly complex symbol which has been said to represent the passage from the profane to the sacred, the journey through the trials of life to the centre of enlightenment. In order to attain enlightenment one may have to overcome the dark side of one's own nature, represented by the monster that may live at the heart of the labyrinth

A Syrio-Hittite stele of the 9th century BC illustrating the exploits of the Mesopotamian hero Gilgamesh, who embarked on a vain quest for the secret of immortality.

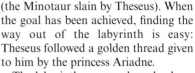

In early Christian theology the path into the labyrinth was regarded as the path of ignorance leading to Hell, with Christ the saviour showing the way out. In some societies, labyrinth designs have been drawn on houses as a form of magic intended to confuse evil spirits and prevent them from entering the home. Graves and burial mounds of labyrinthine design are believed not only to protect the dead but also to prevent their spirits from returning to trouble the living.

(the Minotaur slain by Theseus). When the goal has been achieved, finding the way out of the labyrinth is easy: Theseus followed a golden thread given to him by the princess Ariadne.

The labyrinth or maze has also been interpreted as a mandala, an image of the cosmos used in the East to assist a meditator to find his or her own spiritual focal point or "centre".

A recurrent figure in Irish myth is the hero who voyages to the Otherworld, an ambivalent place of danger and festivity, whose inhabitants know neither age nor death. One, Mael Dúin, encounters ants as big as foals, horse-racing demons and a magical silver net, part of which he lays on the altar of the holy city of Armagh when he returns.

THE HOLY GRAIL

The quest for the Holy Grail was one of the most widespread themes of medieval European epic literature: versions of the story are recorded in almost all the countries of western and northern Europe. Rooted in Celtic myth and the powerful mysteries of early Christianity, the Grail legends explore the theme of spiritual transformation. The Grail itself was reputed to have the ability to confer everlasting life. According to one legend, it was the vessel used by Christ at the Last Supper and the cup in which Joseph of Arimathea caught some of Christ's blood at the Crucifixion. Joseph is said to have wandered abroad with the Grail, eventually carrying it to Britain and the legendary land of Avalon, sometimes identified with Glastonbury in Somerset.

According to French sources dating from the 13th century, the search for the Grail was a spiritual quest undertaken by many of the legendary knights of King Arthur. Three knights, Galahad, Perceval (the Parsifal of German accounts) and Bors, found the Grail in a mysterious city across the sea. Only Galahad looked into the vessel: he died from the ecstasy of his vision.

Today, several esoteric movements use the Grail as a subject for meditation. They regard it as a symbol of the means of attaining spiritual perfection, rather like the alchemical Philosopher's Stone (see p.69).

King Arthur's knights (c.1450).

Pilgrimages

Pilgrims on the Croagh Patrick pilgrimage in Ireland scale the rocky slopes barefoot. Such ordeals recall Christ's journey to Calvary.

Travelling across the landscape toward a certain destination appears in many traditions as a metaphor for the process of inner spiritual growth and the acquisition of knowledge. This is seen in its most literal sense in the act of pilgrimage, in which the physical and spiritual journey are simultaneous. The thousands of people who toil up the slopes of Mount Fuji in Japan, or painfully creep up the steps of a Catholic shrine on their knees, travel the same path of spiritual progress. In doing so they

hope to develop a more complete self and a closer relationship with the divine. The pilgrim leaves the shelter of home and family in order to travel to a place where he or she can encounter some other, superior world, perhaps in the belief that the process will vouchsafe physical or spiritual healing, or divine assistance with personal problems or predicaments. In the ancient Greek world people travelled hundreds of miles to seek counsel from the sacred oracle of Delphi, or to be cured at Epidaurus, at the shrine of the god of healing, Asklepios. Many Christian places of pilgrimage are visited as simple acts of devotion or thanksgiving to a saint, or as penance.

For some, the spiritual value of the pilgrimage increases with the difficulty of the journey, as was demonstrated in 1994 by one Hindu *sadhu* (ascetic) who rolled 200 miles across India – the last 20 miles or so uphill – on a pilgrimage to the shrine of the goddess Devi. Most pilgrim traditions include an element of worldly denial, which is expressed in two landmarks of Christian spiritual literature, *Il Purgatorio* by Dante (1265–1321) and *The Pilgrim's Progress* by John Bunyan (1628–88). In the former work the poet is guided on an otherworldly journey through Purgatory by his beloved

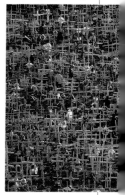

Pilgrims to this Peruvian cemetery leave behind tributes to the dead amid a forest of crosses.

ADAM'S PEAK

A mountain in southwestern Sri Lanka (right), called Samanhela by the Sinhalese, has for centuries been the object of devotion because of its dramatic shape and a strange imprint in the rocky outcrop on its summit. This natural hollow, just under six feet (1.8m) in length, has been interpreted by Buddhists, Muslims, Taoists and Christian visitors as a giant footprint. In Buddhist writings dating from before 300BC it was described as the footprint of the Buddha; Chinese writers have described it as the mark of a god or of their first ancestor; in a Muslim legend it is the footprint that Adam left where he landed after his fall from Paradise. When the Portuguese came to the island in the 16th century they saw it as the footprint of St Thomas.

In order to reach the summit of Adam's Peak, the pilgrim was obliged to traverse steep ravines on steps carved into the rock before climbing a ladder fastened into the cliff face.

According to one legend, the heavy chains on the southwestern face of the mountain are said to have

been placed there by Alexander the Great (365-323BC).

After prayers at the site, each pilgrim rings an ancient bell and takes water from a spring to end the ritual.

Beatrice, who brings him to the Christian view of life itself as pilgrimage. The German churchman Johann Gerhard (1582–1637) wrote in his book of prayers: "Thus I, the object of the world's disdain, with pilgrim face surround the weary earth; I only relish what the world counts vain ... Her freedom is my jail." This world-renouncing spirituality has at times encouraged a negative view of the world, which has come to be seen as a place of exile for humans whose ultimate destination and true home is heaven.

The emphasis in pilgrimage may be on the

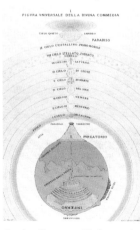

Levels of heaven and hell crossed by the soul in Dante's Divine Comedy.

destination rather than the act of journeying. In Islam, great emphasis is put on the Hajj, the pilgrimage to the holy city of Mecca in Saudi Arabia. The fifth of the religious duties known as the Five Pillars decrees that every Muslim should make the Hajj at least once, unless they are physically incapable, or unless to do so would cause financial hardship to the family.

The idea of a pilgrimage without destination, when the journey travelled is the goal, was expressed somewhat desolately by the American poet Walt Whitman (1819–98), who saw "the universe itself as a road, as many roads, as roads for travelling souls".

Vision quests

An elder of the Cree people emerges from his family sweatlodge. The steam given off heated stones doused with water inside the hut is believed to provide spiritual cleansing and to encourage visions.

The "vision quest" is an ancient practice among indigenous peoples all over the world, including Native Americans, Siberian shamanistic societies and Australian Aboriginals. An individual seeking self-knowledge or spiritual power will enter upon a deliberate ordeal of seclusion, fasting and prayer with the aim of self-purification and in the hope of receiving an ecstatic vision that will show him or her the true path to follow in life.

Once in the "vision state", it is claimed that an individual becomes a disembodied traveller who flies into the heavens and looks back at the Earth and universe. In the quest for truth he or she is said to journey beyond the frontiers of the known world and return bringing

supernatural knowledge and power.

As well as the apparent ascent to heaven, there are other themes common to the vision quests of different cultures. Before returning to the everyday world, the visionary traveller will usually descend to the underworld, confront demonic forces and communicate both with the spirits of the dead and with birds and animals.

Prior to entering the state of ecstasy, visionary travellers may have to go alone into the outside world, away from their group, in order to find a secret place where they can prepare for the vision. The choice of site is important because it must have easy access to the spirit world. Among the Algonkian people of northeastern North America, high cliffs, rock shelters or unusual rock formations are often favoured, as places imbued with spiritual power.

The vision quest often begins at puberty when a boy, or sometimes a girl, asks an elder or medicine man for help in obtaining visions. The seekers receive religious instruction and may participate in rituals in a "sweatlodge", a hut filled with steam into which they retire for purification and healing. They are then taken to an isolated spot to await the vision. The site may be a cleft in a rock, the summit of a hill, or a nest of branches and leaves in a tree. Once there, the initiate must go without food or sleep for a

An artist's vision of transformation during a North American sweatlodge ritual.

day or more until visited by a spirit, often in a dream. Initiates must never divulge the details of their dreams, but they may adopt the symbols of their spirit helper and use them in face paints and decorations, thereby tacitly revealing the helper's identity.

Vision quests may go on throughout life. The Comanche people of the southern Plains of North America believed that a warrior must continue seeking visionary guidance into old age. Pursuing the same visionary path as he did as a youth, he would climb up to a sacred hill with his robe, pipe and tobacco, to smoke, pray and fast in order to be close to the spirit world.

VISION QUESTS OF THE AMERICAN PLAINS

The vision quest of *hanbleceya*, or "crying for a vision", was a sacred rite said to have been given to the Oglala Sioux (Lakota) of the North American Plains by a supernatural being, White Buffalo Calf Woman. The vision seeker is taken to a sacred hill by his spiritual adviser who digs a pit and covers it with brush, marking the four sacred directions with decorated poles and tobacco offerings. The adviser instructs the seeker to take no food or water and to leave the

The Moon as an Above Person*, the medicine shield of Chief Araposh of the Crow people of the Plains, depicts a spirit he met on a vision quest.*

pit only at dawn in order to pray to the Morning Star. During the ordeal, supernatural beings may come to the pit and talk with the seeker, who will experience the visions that will guide him into the future. If an animal or bird comes to him, he may hunt and kill its kind and carry it as war medicine. However, if he dreams of thunder and lightning, he must act out his dream in a ceremony called *heyoka kaga*, or "clown making", in which he shows his new role as a divine fool. His function within the tribe from now on is to do everything idiotically, or backwards.

Land and property

People may define territory broadly in terms of the Earth's own boundaries (oceans, seas, lakes, mountain chains, plateaux and rivers) and more specifically, within these natural confines, in terms of predominant vegetation, fauna, climate, soils or rock type. The borders between such areas are usually undisputed, but when human groups define territory in terms of the settle-

A Pitjantjatjarra elder returns to look after a sacred site in the central deserts of Australia.

ment and culture that have arisen upon it, competing claims almost inevitably occur at some stage between neighbouring groups, and conflict over the precise determination of the frontiers is frequent. National myths arise as part of the process of territorial definition in order to justify the occupation and extent of a group's territories.

In many societies concern about land ownership has tended to focus on the areas associated with small family groups or communities. For example, among the Native American peoples living along the northwest coast of Canada, individual family groups tra-

ditionally owned rights to the area of land that provided them with sufficient shellfish, fish and other food resources. By contrast, foraging rights among Australian Aboriginal tribes are much more loosely defined, and their clan estates are based rather on the guardianship of sacred places and the myths, songs and ceremonies that go with them.

Recent land disputes, such as those in Australia and North America, in which indigenous peoples have confronted the modern political state, demonstrate the difficulty of reconciling the Western concept of land as a commodity, which may be owned and traded, with ancient tribal notions. The Aboriginals, for example, believe that the land was formed by mythological beings during the creation period or Dreaming: as such it is not merely a geological phenomenon but a spiritual one. Human beings may be entrusted with guardianship of ancestral sites associated with the Dreaming, but the idea of land "ownership" is alien: it would mean placing oneself above the sacred spirits of the Dreaming who had created both land and people.

Societies have often drawn consciously on the natural world for emblems of nationhood, and these emblems may themselves express aspects of collective identity. For example, the former Yugoslav republic of Slovenia adopted a stylized view of the Alps as a national symbol on achieving independence in 1991: this expressed the Slovenes' self-reliance as a mountain people and also helped outsiders to locate the new state. Elsewhere, historical events and monuments may be claimed by nations far removed in culture, place or time from the peoples who were originally concerned with them. In Africa the former colonies of Dahomey, Gold Coast and French Sudan adopted the names respectively of Benin, Ghana and Mali, powerful African empires of the pre-colonial period, and Zimbabwe is named after the ruined medieval city of Great Zimbabwe. The adoption of such names not only expressed pride in the achievement of independent statehood, but also helped to instil a sense of national unity within culturally disparate states whose frontiers, drawn by colonizing powers, rarely took account of pre-existing ethnic, cultural or linguistic boundaries.

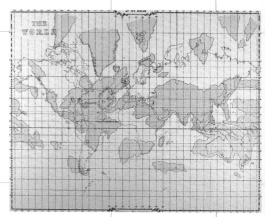

This impression of the primeval world dates from 1896. At this time geographers were fascinated by the myth of Atlantis, the lost continent, a land immune to the claims of empire.

NATIVE LAND IN THE UNITED STATES

In 1787 an ordinance passed by the United States government declared that the native peoples' lands and property would never be taken away from them without consent. However, in 1830 President Andrew Jackson introduced the Indian Removal Act, which compelled all native tribes east of the Mississippi to move west. The Cherokee of Georgia successfully contested the decree in the Supreme Court, but Jackson ignored the decision and the Cherokees were forcibly removed to Oklahoma. More than a quarter of them died on the way.

As the USA expanded, the loss of ancestral lands was vast: the Choctaws alone surrendered more than 10 million acres of their land east of the Mississippi. As native lands were "legally" taken away, their occupants were moved to reservations, often in inhospitable regions with which the displaced peoples had few historical or spiritual connections. In 1887 Native Americans controlled only 138 million acres; by 1934 this was down to 48 million acres, of which nearly half was desert or semi-arid. The massacre by US cavalry of 200 Sioux at Wounded Knee, South Dakota, in 1890, effectively ended armed resistance to the removals.

Columbus, shown here claiming San Salvador island for Spain in 1492, is seen by Native Americans in a distinctly unheroic light.

Dragon haunts

The dragon is one of the most potent symbols of the primordial energy that is the source of all power, both good and evil. In the West, dragon symbolism has tended to emphasize the negative side of that energy, mainly through the influence of Christianity, while Oriental mythology represents the dragon as a positive force, a symbol of the human potential to combine the power of the four elements to creative ends. This distinction is reflected in the way in which each tradition views the relationship between the dragon and the landscape.

In Western mythology, the dragon's

A silk embroidery of a dragon, the sacred emblem of the emperors of China, and the phoenix (above), emblem of the empress.

Chinese dragons, such as this pair on a temple in Hong Kong, are venerated as guardians of the Earth. Unlike the five-clawed imperial dragon they have four claws: in Chinese tradition four is the number of the earth. The earliest Chinese dragons had three claws. It was from these that the Japanese dragon derived – Tatsu, the turbulent spirit of nature, which in its constant conflict with the tiger causes thunderstorms.

association with particular locations is often through its role as a guardian. The dragon is seen as a fearsome, fire-breathing beast that guards treasure (spiritual knowledge) or a maiden (a symbol of purity), and is set up as an obstacle to be overcome by such saintly heroes as St Michael and St George.

In China, the primal power of the dragon was said to be channelled through the landscape along paths of energy, "dragon lines". These lines were regarded as very auspicious locations and used by members of the imperial family as burial sites. Locating the way in which the flow of energy, both positive and negative, interacted with the landscape was developed into a highly sophisticated practice, geomancy (see

ANIMALS AND EARTH

The distinction made between humans and animals in Western traditions is influenced strongly by the Biblical emphasis on the superiority of humankind. However, in many other cultures, people see the rhythm of human life and animal life as interconnected. When a shaman travels mystically in the form of a bear, or an Australian Aborigine decorates himself and dances in imitation of an

ancestral emu from the Dreaming, the act symbolizes the social process of living as part of the Earth, rather than as its master. The role of animals in the life of the Earth is expressed in many origin myths. In Native American and other mythologies, all was endless sea until an animal (such as a muskrat) dived to the bottom of the sea and returned with mud which became the first land.

Hybrid beasts express aspects of our deepest fears.

pp.146–7), which is still used today.

The Chinese dragon is fierce but rarely malevolent: it represents the East, the sun and the bounty of the land. The four-clawed dragon, Mang, represents temporal power. The dragon named Long holds a fiery pearl in its claws, which may represent the moon as a source of fertility, although for Taoists and Buddhists it is the "pearl which grants all desires" (wisdom and enlightenment). As symbols of the dark powers of the Earth, dragons and serpents are close relatives and, in myth, often indistinguishable. The word "dragon" comes from the Greek *dracon*, or large serpent.

In North America, the rock art of the Algonkian people depicts serpents beside natural holes and crevices, perhaps as spiritual messengers to the underworld. In Algonkian myth, the dark side of Earth energy is shown through the great underwater serpent spirit Mizhipichew, which stirs up the

Dragon-slaying heroes appear in many mythologies. This 15th-century Persian miniature shows the hero Rustem and his horse Rakhsh.

waters of lakes with his tail and must be appeased with offerings of tobacco.

In Australia, serpent beings identified with the rainbow bring forth life through the rains and yet are the dangerous guardians of waterholes, easily angered if rituals to propitiate them were not followed correctly.

Animism

According to some philosophies (for example, the Western Newtonian tradition), the physical world is inanimate matter. However, many peoples elsewhere in the world sense that the substance of all earthly things is imbued with spiritual power, and that any object – even a stone or household pot – possesses both a material form and a living essence.

The Melanesian and Polynesian cultures have a concept of *mana* as a force immanent within anything from prized weapons to the personal power of a shaman and his ritual equipment and potions. Aristocratic families are said to possess great *mana*. Until modern times, the most important chiefs in

The symbols painted on this house in the Kalash valley region of northern Pakistan represent protective animal spirits.

Tahiti were never allowed to touch the ground when they travelled, because their *mana* was said to be so powerful that each patch of earth they made contact with would become a sacred place.

A profound reverence for nature lies at the heart of the Shinto religion of Japan. Kami, the divine spirits of Shinto, are everywhere, populating all natural things, especially those with unusual size or form, such as mountains or distinctive trees. They have a profound creative and harmonizing power which can never be fully understood, because it transcends our faculties of cognition.

Native Americans also have a powerful sense of the sacredness of all creation. The Lakota (Sioux) concept of *wakan* refers to a spiritual essence which may reside in a whole range of objects from stones and trees to trade goods: once they called their firearms *maza-wakan*, or "sacred iron". Among the Mi'Kmaq people of Nova Scotia, if someone picks up an unusual stone or some other strange object, it may be prized as having *keskamsit*, or magic good luck, endowed by the creator spirit Kisurgub.

It was once assumed by Westerners that only aboriginal peoples saw the sacred in everything: their perception of a soul (in Latin, *anima*) within mate-

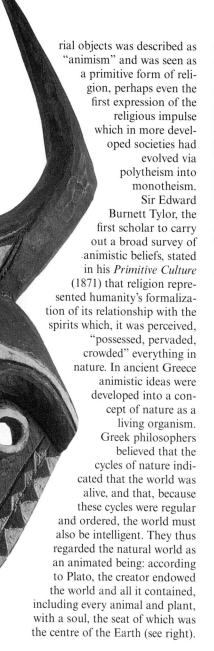

rial objects was described as "animism" and was seen as a primitive form of religion, perhaps even the first expression of the religious impulse which in more developed societies had evolved via polytheism into monotheism. Sir Edward Burnett Tylor, the first scholar to carry out a broad survey of animistic beliefs, stated in his *Primitive Culture* (1871) that religion represented humanity's formalization of its relationship with the spirits which, it was perceived, "possessed, pervaded, crowded" everything in nature. In ancient Greece animistic ideas were developed into a concept of nature as a living organism. Greek philosophers believed that the cycles of nature indicated that the world was alive, and that, because these cycles were regular and ordered, the world must also be intelligent. They thus regarded the natural world as an animated being: according to Plato, the creator endowed the world and all it contained, including every animal and plant, with a soul, the seat of which was the centre of the Earth (see right).

The remains of an animist king – the last to follow the traditional ways – are entombed at Tomok on Samosir Island off Indonesia.

LEFT *The Bapende of Zaïre believe that great power is stored in the heads of animals and wear animal masks in rituals in the belief that they will thereby gain protection from evil.*

ANIMA MUNDI

In his philosophical work *Timaeus*, the Greek philosopher Plato (*c.*427–347BC) provided an account of the origin of the world and of nature which remained influential up until the Renaissance. In this book, Plato developed his concept of the *anima mundi*, or world soul. He described the world as "the fairest and most perfect of intelligible beings, framed like one visible animal comprehending within itself all other animals of a kindred nature".

Members of the 12th-century academic School of Chartres, in France, animated and personified Plato's world soul in their quest to relate the physical world to the sacred. The interest they took in the World Soul arose from their curiosity about creation. The school taught that by observing natural laws and striving to live in harmony with nature, humanity might grow closer to God.

A landscape of relics

The land itself, even where subject to development, continues to preserve the spirit of the past. Woodland, pasture and other managed landscapes preserve a hidden record of complex relationships over time between mankind and topography. Some landscape traces are purely accidental, but no less telling: in a few places in the Canadian prairies, deep ruts left in the soil by the heavy

The idea of a settlement buried by the sands of time is powerfully evocative. Skara Brae, a Neolithic village in the Orkneys, Scotland, came to light in 1850 when a storm stripped away the top of a large sand dune, exposing stone houses.

Red River carts of the first European settlers have survived as reminders of toil, sacrifice and adventure in the New World. However, it is the *constructed* relics of the past that have had most impact on the imagination.

Many landscapes are cultural palimpsests, layered with significance that has accumulated over time. The relics from previous ages – tombs, monuments, temples, ritual constructions of all kinds – provide historians and archaeologists with valuable evidence about our ancestors. A relic in itself, however, is seldom enough to provide the experts with the answers they seek: it is always helpful to interrogate other sources, including documentary evidence. Where this is absent, as it is with prehistoric sites, there is a tendency toward enigma, and this in turn has often generated folklore in pre-scientific times, and controversy in the modern age of academic inquiry.

It is sometimes easy to forget, trapped as we are in our Janus-faced perspective on time, that many peoples in the distant past were also surrounded by relics. A potent image is that of the massive architecture of the Roman empire after its fall, a legacy of aesthetic and engineering sophistication, coupled with all the social and religious contexts that supported it, standing dejectedly amid native settlements that had no use for any of its symbols. Many such survivals have been converted to other uses, and in particular have been plundered for building materials – a fate that has befallen, for example, Stonehenge in southwest England.

Abandoned ruins become the focus for a localized form of mythmaking. In Europe their appeal finds expression in Romantic ghost stories and tragedies that take place in evocative ruined castles and abbeys, as well as in the gardens and parks of the English Picturesque movement. The urge to fabricate a relic has led to countless follies (using the term in its architectural sense) and literary forgeries, and also, arguably, to the whole tradition of European classicism with its simulated temples and pediments.

The image of an ideal landscape in the late 18th and early 19th centuries, as shown in this painting by William Marlow (1740–1813), was saturated with classical references, especially Picturesque ruins.

THE *MARY ROSE*

Relics recovered from the sea have a special resonance, and it would not be too far-fetched to suggest that this is partly to do with the sense of re-birth, the miraculous recovery of the irretrievable.

The *Mary Rose* was built at Portsmouth on the south coast of England in 1509–10 for the royal fleet of King Henry VIII. She was a warship with seven heavy bronze guns and 34 heavy iron guns. In 1513, after Sir Edward Howard used her during engagements with the French, he described the *Mary Rose* to the King as "your good ship, the flower I trow of all ships that ever

sailed". On July 19, 1545, she sailed out to face a large French fleet in the Solent off Portsmouth. After turning sharply during a brisk offshore breeze, she heeled, took on water through her gun ports and sank like a stone, taking more than 650 men with her.

Efforts were made to salvage the *Mary Rose* after the tragedy. However, none was successful, and she soon settled on her starboard side into the mud of the Solent, gradually lost her masts, and was forgotten.

Over the next 400 years, shifting mud exposed the blackened stumps of several ribs of the vessel. Salvagers found her this way in 1836

and then archaeologists rediscovered her in 1971. The remains of the hull were lifted in 1982.

Divers probed the English Channel mud to find the wreck of the Mary Rose.

Earth Energy

From the highest mountains in the
Himalayas to Ireland's holy springs, features
of the landscape have been recognized by
initiates as places where the Earth's spiritual
pulse is most strongly felt. This notion of the
planet's energy is an extension of such
empirically known phenomena as gravity
and magnetism. The proven efficacy of
dowsing and similar techniques conjures
even for many Western sceptics a realm of
quasi-electrical impulses within or beneath
the Earth's crust. In many traditions,
intimations of Earth energy have been overtly
spiritualized. An adept might retire to a
mountain peak, a waterfall or a cave in order
to enter the force-field of the otherworld,
believing that the energy encountered there
will provide aid in the quest, and inner
strength for the journey into the world of
the spirit.

*Vast moving landscapes of deep gullies and mountainous waves
unfurl themselves across the sea. Thermal currents (heating at
the Equator and cooling at the poles), winds, tides and the
"Coreolis effect" (a function of the Earth's rotation) keep the
oceans in perpetual motion.*

Waters of life

As water is essential to all life, its frequent association with spiritual and creative power has an obvious logic. Consecrated water is often used in rituals as a medium to bring about or symbolize a spiritual awakening, and baptism of one form or another is widely practised as a rite of passage. To pass through water as a symbolic act of

A great waterfall such as Iguazú Falls, Brazil, excites the senses with its thunderous display.

death and rebirth is commonly part of initiation rites marking the beginning of adulthood. The initiation rite of the Yolngu people of northern Australia re-enacts the swallowing and regurgitation of two boys by Yurlunggur, a great serpent venerated as the source of rain.

In Christian baptism, a new person is believed to arise from the waters, reborn within the body of the Church and the spirit of Christ. In early Christian societies baptism often

Baptists perform baptismal rites in a temporary pool specially erected at Wembley Stadium, London.

involved total immersion in streams and rivers, but by the 4th century the Church had introduced the practice of baptizing by trickling "holy water" over the forehead from a font blessed with the sign of the cross.

The baptismal rite consciously parallels Christ's own death and resurrection, which, according to Christian theology, was prefigured in the Old Testament story of Jonah and the whale. Jonah was in flight from God until his ordeal in the belly of the "great fish", a symbol of the transfiguring energy of the cosmic waters of creation.

Ritual bathing has a physical as well as a spiritual function: we cleanse our bodies, as we wash away our sins. Worshippers often touch themselves with water or wash before entering a sacred place, a practice shared, among many others, by ancient Greeks and modern Muslims. The ritual bathing of sacred objects is performed with similar intent. The Greeks bathed statues of their goddesses every year in order to reaffirm their powers. The king of Saudi Arabia performs an annual ritual washing of the Ka'ba stone, the sacred black rock which stands as the focal point of the Muslim holy city of Mecca, of which he is the guardian.

Water surrounding a place, contained in a dyke, moat or ditch, offers physical protection, but is also traditionally believed to form a sacred enclosure, ensuring that the inner space remains pure.

The primal power of water is seen in the ancient volcanic landscape of Yellowstone National Park, Wyoming, which roars with sulphurous geysers and boiling mud, while steam rises from hot river basins. Cutting through this violent landscape, the Yellowstone River endlessly erodes the mountains.

A relief of the goddess Ishtar on a lion from Tel Asmar, Iraq, 8th century BC.

ISHTAR AND DUMUZI

Water plays a significant role in the ancient Akkadian story of the goddess Ishtar's descent to the underworld. The tale was first recorded in Bronze Age texts and later inscribed on clay tablets in the palace library built in the late 8th century BC at Nineveh, the capital of the Assyrian empire.

When Ishtar, the Mesopotamian goddess of love, fertility and war, forces her way into the underworld, she is stripped of her powers and treated as one of the dead, a situation which causes great problems on Earth. Only when Namtar, the goddess's vizier, goes to the entrance of the underworld and sprinkles Ishtar with the waters of life can she return.

The story of Ishtar's return to life on earth ends with instructions for the ritual treatment of a statue of Ishtar's lover, the god Dumuzi, who is forced to spend half of each year in the underworld: in order that his image may lie in state in Nineveh during the *taklimtu* fertility festival, it is to be washed with pure water and clothed in a red burial cloth.

Water from the Earth

In many traditions the source of the sweet waters that issue from the earth as springs, wells, and waterfalls is the supernatural underworld. Wells and springs are often said to represent the spiritual womb of the Earth and to possess the power to heal, confer wisdom or grant wishes. At Bath in England (see p.56), archaeologists have found hundreds of "curse tablets" – imprecations scratched on lead and thrown into the sacred spring of the Romano-British deity Sulis-Minerva, goddess of wisdom. In the symbolic imagination of the Zuñi people of the southwestern United States, springs are joined to the distant oceans like the runners of willows to a single plant. According to Zuñi origin myths, the Daylight People, the first humans, emerged into this world through the waters of a spring from the underworld below.

A multiple waterfall issuing from a rock, in the Gental, near Bern, Switzerland.

As a source of life, springs and wells often act as symbols of love and marriage, sexuality and procreation. Nymphs and fairies are widely believed to frequent their waters, beguiling lovers and strangers and giving rise to the notion of wishing wells. The Tsimshian people of the northwestern coast of North America, relating how light came to the world, describe how the light-bringer Raven transformed himself into a leaf at a spring where the daughter of the chief of heaven came to drink. The chief's daughter then swallowed the leaf and became pregnant, eventually giving birth to Raven in his human form.

Throughout the world, many sacred wells are said to have the power to make barren women fertile; closed wells, on the other hand, symbolize virginity.

Because springs and wells are often alleged to provide openings to the underworld they are sometimes seen as dangerous places. According to ancient Irish mythology, for instance, the hero

Frank Lloyd Wright's design for his house Fallingwater, Pennsylvania (1936), echoed the natural patterns of the nearby waterfalls.

ETERNAL YOUTH

The quest for a fountain or spring that would ensure eternal youth occurs in many traditions. The Coyote of North America relate how the Creator was about to bring humanity into being and summoned two buzzards to build a ladder to heaven. He told them to make two springs at the top, one for drinking, the other for bathing. Whenever an old person reached the top and used the springs, their youth would be restored. The buzzards began their task but the trickster Coyote pointed out that if people always had the promise of youth they would eternally climb up and down the ladder, without making friends or families. The buzzards saw he was right and destroyed their work.

The fountain in the Garden of Youth, as depicted by a 15th-century Italian artist.

Diarmaid grappled with a wizard at a magic well and fell into its depths, emerging in a supernatural land peopled with new adversaries.

There is an important group of holy wells in Ireland, exemplified by the Otherworld well of Seghais, which is interpreted as the source of the two

Villagers in Derbyshire, England, "dress" wells in springtime to purify them.

great rivers the Boyne and the Shannon. Myths about the well tell of a beautiful woman who guarded it, whose favour was sought by visiting warrior chieftains: sexual intercourse with the woman was symbolically identified with drinking from the well and attaining wisdom. Around the site are nine hazel trees, whose magic nuts supposedly dropped into the well to cause "bubbles of inspiration". A supernatural salmon in the well ate the hazel nuts, thereby becoming the Salmon of Wisdom (*eo fis*). Anyone who can catch and eat this salmon becomes endowed with bardic powers.

Holy wells are also found in Wales, some with healing properties, others used as cursing wells. An example of the latter is St Aelian's Well at Llanelian yn Rhos, whose cult flourished in the early 19th century: the victim's initials would be scratched on a tablet of slate, or written on parchment sealed with lead, and placed inside the well. The idea recalls the curse tablets used by the Romans at Bath (see above).

Bath, southwest England

For at least 10,000 years hot mineral springs have
gushed from the ground at the site of Bath, the point
where a low clay ridge rises above the River Avon,
Somerset, on one of its meanders through the Cots-
wold hills. The ancient Britons recognised the curative
properties of the springs, which were sacred to Sulis, a
goddess of water and healing whose name derives
from the Celtic word for "sun": it has been suggested
that this refers to the heat of the springs.

The Romans identified Sulis with the goddess Minerva as a healing deity. Around AD70 they transformed the main spring, which they called Aquae Sulis
("Waters of Sulis"), into a temple complex with baths
for pilgrims and those seeking cures. Worshippers
prayed to the goddess Sulis-Minerva for healing, protection and the punishment of malefactors. Other
deities were worshipped at Bath, including a triad of
Celtic Earth mother goddesses, the Suleviae (see p.19).

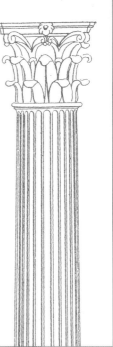

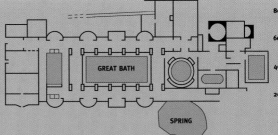

The Roman bath, lined with
lead from the Mendip hills, was
rediscovered in 1755, but was
not fully excavated and rebuilt
(above) until the 1880s.

The plan of the Roman baths
of Sulis Minerva (above)
shows the original spring to
the north of the complex (at
the bottom of this picture). In
the centre is the main bath.
The goddess's temple, an
austere building with a
pediment supported on four
Corinthian columns (right),
stood to the northwest of the
old spring.

The building of the Pump Room in 1790, during Bath's heyday as a spa resort, drew attention to the presence of extensive Roman remains in the city centre. An antiquarian, James Levine, began to explore the area in the 1860s, and the open-air Roman bath seen today was fully exposed during the 1880s. Finds from the sacred spring and culvert include thousands of coins and many inscribed leaden "curse tablets". The tablets provide textual evidence that many visitors asked the goddess Sulis-Minerva for help in recovering possessions or punishing enemies and thieves. It is unclear whether gifts of coins referred to in the texts were thrown into the spring or given to attendant priests.

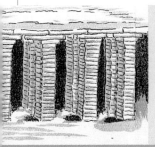

A detail from a British Museum manuscript of 1888 showing the construction of the baths. It is a cross-section illustrating the Roman hypocaust system of underfloor central heating, almost universal in villas and public buildings in the colder provinces, in which floors were supported on tiles to allow hot air from a furnace to circulate and heat the building above.

The central feature of the main temple pediment, found at the end of the 18th century, is a fine bearded male head which fuses Celtic and Graeco-Roman traditions: it resembles Celtic gods of fertility and healing but is clearly based on classical representations of the female Gorgon Medusa, whose severed head was worn by Minerva to turn her enemies to stone.

The sacred status of Bath was still recognized 500 years after the Romans departed: King Edgar, the first ruler of all England, was crowned here in AD973. The springs were used in the medieval period, but it was only in the 17th and 18th centuries that Bath developed as a fashionable spa resort. The social focus of the spa was the King's Bath, shown here in an illustration of 1675.

Rivers and streams

A river is an ancient and widespread metaphor for the course of human life, from birth, conception or previous existence (the source) to death, the afterlife or reincarnation (the river's outlet to the sea). In Buddhist thought, the river of life must be traced back to its source in order to attain enlightenment.

More generally, the parodoxical image of a river flowing upstream represents the return to a pristine, paradisal state of being.

For the ancient civilizations that depended on irrigation, rivers were major symbols of fruitfulness and contentment – as in the image of the four rivers of paradise flowing from the Tree of Life to the cardinal points.

Rivers and streams may form the boundary between life and death, the most famous example being Styx and Acheron, the rivers of Hades. In Japanese Buddhist and Shinto teaching the Sanzunokawa river is said to separate the dead from the living. Rivers also divide the visible world from magical regions such as the Otherworld of old Slav tradition, which has often been envisaged as lying on the far shore of a fiery river.

Rivers are often regarded as sacred, and may even be seen as deities in their own right. The Tigris and Euphrates were worshipped by the ancient Hittites, and the Yoruba of West Africa believe that the river Ogun is the transformed goddess Yemoja. Whereas the Earth is often seen as a goddess, river water is sometimes viewed as the body of a god. In a deluge story told by the Ifugao people of the Philippines, the elders treated a dried-up river as dead and in its grave; as they dug to find its soul, they opened a great gushing spring that soon covered the Earth.

Supernatural beings are also believed to reside in rivers. For example, among

The boatman Charon ferries the dead across the Styx to the shores of the underworld.

Sailing boats journey into eternity in the tomb of Sennufer at Thebes, Egypt, c.1567–1320BC.

the Finno-Ugric tribal peoples of northwestern Europe water spirits are at once annoying tricksters, evil demons and providers of fish and other food resources. The Votjaks of Russia call the festival of Twelfth Night "the following of the water spirit". The morning after the festivities people may throw offerings of meat, bread or porridge into the river or sacrifice a duck in order to appease the spirit and ensure a ready supply of food.

The great Hindu pilgrimages are focused on sacred rivers, particularly the Ganges, which is venerated as a goddess, Ganga (see pp. 62–3). Some pilgrims take water from its source in the foothills of the Himalayas and pour it on the linga (phallic obelisk) at Ramesvaram, a village two thousand miles to the south. In so doing they are uniting the sacred essence of the goddess Ganga with the symbol of Shiva, bringing together the female river goddess and the male god of fertility.

Like all waters, rivers are both dangerous and nurturing, as seen in those great rivers which seasonally flood but deposit a rich layer of silt when they subside. The Nile in Egypt, the Tigris and Euphrates in Mesopotamia and the Indus in India provided, literally, the fertile soil for the first civilizations.

RIVER BURIALS

Burial rites have been performed on sacred rivers in many parts of the world. Across Europe, folktales and legends also refer to human sacrifices being made by rivers and at sacred springs.

The LoDagaa of northern Ghana throw the bodies of those who have died spiritually unclean deaths into rivers in order to cleanse the community.

In India, the act of scattering ashes on the holy waters of the Ganges permits the soul of the deceased to bathe in the body of the goddess Ganga. The point at which the Ganges meets its first tributary, the Yamuna (Jumna), is a particularly sacred place. The ashes of Mahatma Gandhi, the great spiritual and political leader, were scattered at this spot.

In China the souls of the drowned were thought to haunt rivers, looking for living bodies they could occupy.

Cremated bodies on the Ganges, the holiest of Hinduism's seven most sacred rivers.

The Ganges, India

The Ganges is the spiritual artery of India. It is regarded as the personification of the goddess Ganga, who is said to have descended to earth after King Bhagiratha pleased the gods with years of worship in the Himalayas. To prevent the crashing waters from causing a disaster on earth, Lord Shiva meditating on Mount Kailasa supposedly caught the river in his hair. With the onset of the monsoon season in mid-June each year, the story of the river's descent from heaven is celebrated in the festival of Ganga-dussera.

The heavenly origin of the Ganges makes its water holy as the essence of the goddess, or female energy, known as *shakti*. Drinking water from the Ganges and bathing in it are therefore sacred rituals. People from all over India converge on Rishikesh, the first settlement after the river's course through the Himalayas, and Hardwar, a town farther south where the water is believed to be holiest. Varanasi (Benares) is sacred as Shiva's city. Hiuen Tsiang, a Buddhist pilgrim who trekked overland from China to India in the 7th century AD, witnessed "hundreds and thousands" of people cleansing themselves on the ghats at Hardwar. Many people still travel there in order to fill their pots and jars with Ganges water which they consume at weddings and funerals.

Although dams now control parts of the Ganges, harnessing energy and preventing floods, the river still carries prayers, offerings and ashes to the sea.

The Ganges begins at Gomukh (above), more than 13,000 feet (4,200m) up in the Himalayas below the peak of Shivalinga. This is a holy place where pilgrims may hear the voices of spirits created by the winds rushing across the face of the ice. The ice stream flows down the mountain, joining with other sources until it finally becomes the great river.

The stone landings and steps, together with gilded temples and palaces, stretch for four miles (6km) along the Ganges at Varanasi (above) in order to accommodate the many pilgrims to this sacred place. Smoke from cremations on special ghats drifts along the river as pilgrims bathe.

For the pilgrims who flock to its shores, the Ganges offers the hope of a better future. At sunset, temple bells ring out and people launch boats of leaves filled with flower petals and lighted candles into the waters of the Ganges in the hope that they will carry their prayers to the heavens.

Fishing boats are often seen on the Ganges, except around Hardwar where fish are considered sacred.

The Ganges passes through an astounding series of transformations on its 1,500-mile (2,507km) journey through India. The river flows swiftly at first, cutting through gorges in the mountains; it then wanders across a broad flat plain where it is used for irrigation, until finally it empties into the Bay of Bengal by way of the largest delta in the world.

The Kumbh Mela festival is held every 12 years, when the sun, moon and stars are in a particular alignment in the Hindu zodiac. Bathing in the Ganges brings especially good luck at this time, and so millions of pilgrims make the journey to Allahabad, the city on the banks of the Ganges in northern India where the festival is held.

Seas and lakes

Sacred lakes were an important part of the temple complexes of Thebes, at Karnac and Luxor. Above is the sacred lake of Amun.

The sea is the ancestral origin of life – formless, inexhaustible, latent with potential. It is also a maternal image of great power, a metaphor for unfathomable wisdom and, in psychology, a symbol of the unconscious.

Oceans can transform themselves from calm to frenzy within a matter of minutes. All maritime cultures tend to view them as a source of plenty, but also as an environment beset with dangers – not only storms, but also threats lurking in an otherworld below the water's surface.

In Norse myth, the oceans were the blood of the giant primordial being Ymir, and ancient legends speak of giant sea goddesses, Hafgygr and Margygr, who wrecked ships. Early European maps of the world often picture sea monsters in the oceans, inspired by the wildly imaginative accounts of seafarers.

The hold of the sea on all who live beside it is captured in the sombre stories fisherfolk tell of the spirits that haunt their daily lives. According to the Estonians, a version of the Baltic water spirit Nåkk sometimes appeared as a horse galloping along the seashore, enticing children to ride him to their doom in the waves. On other occasions, the same spirit would bewitch the eyes of his victims so that they were unable to tell the land from the sea and so were lured to their deaths.

Lakes in myth are often an occult medium, linked (especially in Arthurian legends) with female enchantment, and with death, the abyss and the night passage of the sun (from observation of its apparent disappearances into water).

The sea monsters on this 18th-century map of Africa symbolize the physical and spiritual dangers encountered by sailors.

THE DEAD SEA

Situated in the middle of a desert, the Dead Sea is, as the name suggests, an eerie, lifeless place which, through the Hebrew Scriptures, has taken on the symbolism of a spiritual wilderness. It is in fact a landlocked salt lake lying about 1,300 feet (400m) below sea level, with summer temperatures rising to well over 40°C (104°F). The only life forms able to survive in its extremely salty waters are a few bacteria and specially adapted plants. Evaporation and the variable flow of the rivers that feed the lake cause its water level to rise and fall by up to 2 feet (0.6m). As a result, salt is deposited, creating an undulating landscape of salt mounds and pillars.

The Biblical cities of Sodom and Gomorrah are believed to have been situated on the lake's southern shore, and its bleak, salt-encrusted landscape was drawn on for the account of their destruction. Unwilling to punish the only virtuous people in Sodom, Lot and his family, God allowed them to escape on condition that they never looked back. When Lot's wife stole a parting glance, she was turned into a pillar of salt.

Indirectly, the Dead Sea has been the inspiration for a more modern ideology. The ancient Hebrew and Arabic manuscripts known as the Dead Sea Scrolls were discovered in caves close to the lake. Some believe them to have been the work of the Essenes, a sect which flourished about 2,000 years ago. The interest of the Essenes today stems in part from the claim that their lives were in step with the natural world and recognized the sacred unity of all life on Earth.

The Dead Sea, the lowest point on the Earth's surface, lies saturated with salt.

THE LADY OF THE LAKE

The Lady of the Lake, a prophetess with magical powers, is first mentioned in Arthurian legend in the *Conte de la charette* by Chrétien de Troyes (1179). She appears as the guardian of the knight Lancelot and the forger of his sword: she gives him a magic ring, set with a stone that enables him to break spells, as well as a white lance which can penetrate steel. She is the opponent of the enchantress Morgan Le Fay. Also, under various names (Viviane, Niniane and, in Sir Thomas Malory's *Le Morte Darthur*, Nemué), she is the lover of Merlin, whom she imprisons in a tree, tomb or cave.

In some versions, she sees the future but declines to prophesy as this would result in more people dying.

The romances disagree about her precise dwelling-place, variously depicted as the sea, a place beyond the sea, a lake isle, or a place beneath the mirage of a lake.

Her court is made up entirely of women (except for Lancelot), and this echoes the Celtic notion of the Otherworld as a Land of Women. The Lady's role as giver of Arthur's sword is found only in Malory.

In Malory's version, the Lady of the Lake thrust up her arm to offer Arthur his magic sword. She reclaimed it as he lay dying by the lakeside.

Stone

Ayers Rock (Uluru), a sandstone outcrop, is one of the most sacred sites for Aboriginal Australians.

From the perspective of a human lifetime, rock has seemed to possess an immovable, eternal nature. This may explain its association, in many cultures, with the supernatural and the divine. Rock stores heat, cold, water and (as gemstones) light, and much of its symbolism comes from these properties, and from its unyielding solidity. Its sacredness is reflected not only in prehistoric megaliths but also in its use for objects such as amulets and for sacrificial knives.

Kissing the stone at Castle Blarney, Ireland.

Supernatural beings are often said to reside in rocks. The Sami of northern Russia believe that certain unusual stones known as *seite* are inhabited by spirits that control the surrounding animals. One account of 1671 describes a ritual in which the spirit within the *seite* was propitiated by a reindeer sacrifice in order to ensure good hunting. In the forests of northern Russia, the hunting and gathering Tungus people believe that a dangerous spirit of the woods, the Forest Master, can take the form of a rock, and they avoid any rock which resembles a human or animal for fear of disturbing him. Elsewhere, small rocks or stones are sometimes piled up and viewed as representations of a deity: in the south of India, rocks heaped in village shrines are regarded as the *ammas*, local goddesses who guard villages.

Stones themselves are widely believed to have sacred or magical properties, and prayers or offerings are often made at prominent or strangely formed outcrops associated with spirit energy. In Brittany and elsewhere, ancient standing stones and other monoliths are traditionally believed to contain the power to make barren women fertile. Those who succeed in kissing a particular stone at Blarney Castle, Ireland, are said to receive the gift of eloquence (see illustration, opposite); this idea is based on the oracular symbolism of stone, not only in Celtic tradition but elsewhere too. Small, painted stones decorated in prehistoric times and discovered at the foot of rock painting sites in western Canada may have been charms: the use of stones as talismans is found almost everywhere.

Travellers dancing, presided over by a herm, an obelisk representing the Greek god Hermes.

In ancient Greece, people would traditionally leave piles of small stones on top of herms, the often phallic, roadside obelisks that represented the god Hermes, patron deity of communication and travellers. In doing so they hoped to win the god's favour or protection on their journey.

Stones may become powerful spiritual symbols for a tribe or nation. At Delphi in Greece, a carved stone marked the omphalos, the centre of the world (see pp. 24–5 and 88–9). Scottish kings were enthroned at Scone in Fife on a sacred "stone of destiny" which was reputed to be the stone on which the patriarch Jacob laid his head when he dreamed of the destiny of the Israelites. Legend has it that the stone reached Scone after being carried from the Near East to Ireland, the original homeland of the Scots, where it was first used in enthronement rituals. When King Edward I of England (who ruled 1272–1307) defeated the Scots, he moved the stone to London, where it was incorporated into a new coronation throne to symbolize his subjugation of Scotland.

The coronation chair in Westminster Abbey, London, with the stone of Scone, removed from Scotland in 1296 by Edward I, beneath the seat.

Stones from deep space and time

Meteors are scraps of rocky space débris which disintegrate in the Earth's atmosphere. Larger pieces may fall to Earth as meteorites. Here, the track of a burning meteor is clearly visible.

Stones that fall from the sky represent a unique visitation from the heavens and are often regarded as charged with spiritual energy. The impact of meteorites on the imagination is demonstrated by the extent to which they feature in religious beliefs. According to some accounts, the Persian god of light, Mithra, whose cult became popular throughout the Roman Empire,

Muslims circle the Ka'ba (centre) seven times at the start and end of the pilgrimage to Mecca.

emerged from a burning cosmic rock that was probably a meteorite. The cult of the Earth mother goddess Cybele, centred on Pergamum in Asia Minor (modern Turkey), had as its focal point of worship a silver statue which encased a small black stone, almost certainly a meteorite. The statue was considered so powerful that in 204BC, on the direction of the Delphic oracle, it was carried to Rome in the belief that it would aid the Romans in their war against Carthage.

Millions of Muslims have a sacred duty to make a pilgrimage to Mecca to pay homage at the Grand Mosque to the Ka'ba , the most sacred shrine of Islam. Built into a corner of the Ka'ba is the Hajaru 'l-Aswad or Black Stone, which is thought to be a meteorite and was supposedly brought down to Earth by the archangel Gabriel. Pilgrims walk around the Ka'ba seven times before entering the shrine and kissing or touching the stone.

Rocks of terrestrial origin are often associated with the sky. In Africa, the

Numana people of the River Niger region worship small pebbles which they believe to be pieces of the sky god that have fallen to Earth. The pebbles are placed on top of cones of earth and sacrifices are offered to them.

Fossils of ammonites, which became extinct 66 million years ago, occur worldwide.

Stones bearing the fossils of plants or animals provide evidence of evolution, but even before the scientific age they were objects of fascination. Prehistoric peoples were undoubtedly struck by their unusual appearance, since it is not uncommon to find them at prehistoric sites, sometimes deliberately incorporated into stone artefacts. The mystery of fossils is still strong in societies isolated from scientific discovery. For example, belemnites, fossils of the pen-shaped bodies of a squid-like creature which are found on beaches in the Baltic Sea, are regarded by some Finno-Ugric tribal peoples as the fingers of a water spirit.

Fossils may also be treated as sacred objects. In a well-digging ceremony in Indonesia, a ritual marriage is performed for an ammonite, a fossil of a shell-fish held sacred to the gods, and a basil plant, representing a garden – a union believed to keep the waters sweet and flowing.

The Wolf Creek Crater, made by a meteor, in Western Australia, just over half a mile long.

THE PHILOSOPHER'S STONE

In popular belief, the "philosopher's stone" was an elusive substance sought by alchemists in order to turn ordinary metals into gold. However, the true aim of alchemy was more profound: the discovery of the divine medium (not necessarily a stone) that could effect the transformation of spirit and matter into a state of

A 19th-century view of an alchemist turning lead to gold.

ultimate perfection. The physical transmutation of metals was simply an indicator providing the alchemist with a way of knowing that he had discovered the transforming medium. Jung regarded alchemy as a paradigm for the development of human nature. He saw the philosopher's stone as a psychological process: the transformative experience of self-realization, or individuation.

Rock formations and outcrops

Geometrically regular rock formations are often credited with supernatural origins. This volcanic outcrop in California is called Devil's Post Pile.

Prominent outcrops of rock feature significantly in the mythologized landscape of many cultures. For hunting and gathering peoples they may be the places where supernatural ancestors went about their daily tasks. Sometimes markings in the rock are identified as footprints or other human traces, and taken as proof of an ancestral being's passing. In the plains of South Dakota the Sioux left offerings of tobacco and beads on an exposed rock supposedly bearing human footprints, and the Australian ancestral beings Djanggawul and his two sisters were believed to have had sexual organs so long that they dragged along the ground when they walked during the Dreaming, leaving permanent marks on the landscape.

It is often believed that spirit beings actually inhabit strange rock formations. For example, the Aboriginal peoples of northern Australia claim that a race of supernatural trickster beings, the *mimi*, live in cracks in the cliff face of the Arnhem Land escarpment. In North America the ochre image of a horned figure painted by the Algonkians on Painted Rock Channel at the Lake of Woods is believed to represent a rock-dwelling spirit being similar to the Ojibwa *maymaygwayshiwuk* (see opposite), who were believed by some to be the painters of the red ochre images found across Ojibwa country.

In some places, the rocks themselves are regarded as animals, humans or supernatural beings that have been transformed into stone. In the Kyushu district of Japan, a stone formation set high on the cliffs of the hills of Matsuura is seen as a lady of the royal court, turned to stone as she watched her husband sail off on an expedition to Korea in AD457. She still stands there, leaning forward with her dress trailing behind her, gazing after the disappearing ship. In the Western Kimberley mountains of northwestern Australia the Aboriginals view an entire rock formation as the *wandjina*, the ancestors of the Araluli people, who are believed to have been turned to stone as they stood fishing for rock cod. The Judeo-Christian tradition recounts how the wife of Lot was turned into a pillar of salt during the family's flight from the destruction of Sodom: slender salt rock outcrops are a notable feature of the area in which the Biblical story is set (see p.65).

High rock outcrops are commonly seen as places close to the heavens, and as such they may be revered as the home of divinities. Examples include Spider Rock in Canyon de Chelly, Arizona (see pp.74–5), and the numerous outcrops in Europe dedicated to the god Apollo or the archangel Michael (see pp.146–7).

The Giant's Causeway, a natural basalt formation on the coast of Co. Antrim, Northern Ireland. According to ancient Irish mythology it was built by the hero Finn mac Cumhaill (the Scottish Fingal) as a causeway across the sea to Fingal's Cave, a similar geological phenomenon on Staffa in the Hebrides.

SPIRITS OF THE ROCKS

Many Native Americans believe that certain rocks are inhabited by tiny spirit beings. The Ojibwa Indians of the Great Lakes region call these beings the *maymaygwayshiwuk*. They live in the crevices of the cliffs which line the lakeshores, whence they might creep out to steal fishing gear or play other tricks on travellers.

The Mi'Kmaq of Nova Scotia tell of a similar being called the *hamaja'lu*. In one tale, a group of travellers discovers the *hamaja'lu* tapping away at rocks and making pictures. On closer examination, the travellers find that the pictures are of themselves. The Seneca of New York State perform a ritual in honour of rock-dwelling little people who allegedly once helped a young Seneca man who had wandered into their home.

The naming of rocks often reflects a deep-seated anthropomorphizing tendency. This rock pillar on the coast of Hoy in the Orkneys, Scotland, is know as the "Old Man". It was formed by the erosive action of the sea at the base of a small headland, which eventually caused a section of the headland to collapse.

Caves and crevices

Openings into the body of the Earth, by their nature dark and mysterious, elicit widely differing emotions. Some see them as damp, airless and claustrophobic, infested with bats and other night creatures. No one, it is believed, would choose to live in such an environment, unless compelled to, as Paleolithic peoples are believed to have been in their attempt to shelter from the elements and barricade themselves against fierce animals. Others respond more positively to their ancient and numinous connotations.

It is often assumed that Paleolithic cave artists held nature in awe and penetrated the darkness in search of spiritual enlightenment. However, the fear

Early Christian monks hollowed out cliffs and cone-shaped mounds in the Cappadocia region of Anatolia in order to make cells and chapels.

of caves and crevices could well be a purely modern phenomenon. To early peoples, they may have offered the promise of shelter and comfort in their womb-like passages and clefts. People accustomed to living in a world without artificial light may have felt at ease in total darkness.

At night, bats and other nocturnal creatures spill out of the mouth of a jungle-shrouded cave in Borneo.

Nevertheless, it is probable that caves prompted contrasting emotions, and that these found expression in beliefs about creation and death. Myths of emergence often take place at caves or openings in the Earth – settings suggestive of birth. A cave shrine on Mount Ida in Crete is one of the sites claimed as the birthplace of Zeus; and, according to the Anyanja tribal group from southern Africa, all humans and animals emerged from a hole in the ground at a place called Kapirimtiya, east of Lake Nyasa, leaving their footprints in a rock.

However, caves also lead to the gloomy regions of the underworld, land of the dead. Gilgamesh, the legendary Mesopotamian hero-king of the 2nd millennium BC, was compelled to travel more than twelve leagues through a dark and terrifying passage into the depths of Mount Mashu before he eventually reached the subterranean home of the sun.

Fertility symbolism associated with caves and dwarf rain gods appears in Mexico. In China caves were sacred burial places for emperors, who were reborn from them.

The prehistoric Anasazi people of the southwestern United States built brick villages in the crevices of cliffs. Cliff Place in Colorado, shown here, has more than 200 rooms and 23 ceremonial chambers.

CAVES IN MESOAMERICAN BELIEF

The cave played an important part in Mesoamerican belief and ritual. The sun and moon were said to have been formed in a cave, and the first Nahua people were believed to have emerged from the ground at a place known as Chicomoztoc, or "the place of the seven caves". Some researchers have identified Chicomoztoc with Arizona, and have suggested that the Nahua people were distantly related to the prehistoric Anasazi people of Arizona who inhabited the natural caves found in cliff faces (see pp.74–5).

As in many cultures, caves were used as natural shrines to gods and earth spirits. The Aztec god Centeotl was allegedly born in a cavern, and cotton and edible plants were said to have grown from different parts of his body. Tlaloc, the god of rain and earth, was honoured with the yearly sacrifice of four children who were sealed in a cave, and inside the Yopico pyramid at Tenochtitlan the flayed skins of sacrificial victims were placed in an artificial cave as offerings to a vegetation god.

Such was the perceived power of the cave that it influenced the choice of site for the Pyramid of the Sun, the most important monument in Teotihuacan, the pre-Aztec "city of the gods". Built in the 1st century BC, the pyramid was set directly over an earlier sacred place, an underground cave and shrine. The inhabitants hoped that, through the choice of such a location, the ancient power of the Earth would be harnessed to the new monument as it reached up toward the sky.

In Inca belief, too, caves play a prominent role. According to the Inca origin myth, the ancestors of the Inca people – three brothers and three sisters – emerged from a group of three caves at Pacariqtambo ("the place of origin"), near Cuzco.

Canyon de Chelly, Arizona

Canyon de Chelly cuts deeply into the red sandstone beds of Defiance Plateau in northeastern Arizona. It was formed by a large desert wash that flows out of the Tunicha Mountains, winding sinuously until it disappears in juniper and sagebrush flats almost 30 miles (50km) away. The canyon walls have been sculpted by weathering into a myriad of spectacular shapes, from sheer cliff faces to voluptuous mounds and hollows.

In places where large areas of rock have broken away to create low shelters, an ancient agrarian people named the Anasazi were able to take mud mortar, stones and sticks and build multi-storied dwellings which clung to the canyon walls. Some of these settlements could be reached only with the help of ladders or precarious footholds driven into the rock. The Anasazi also painted and engraved images – animals, human-like figures, spirals and other geometric designs – in caves or rock shelters throughout the canyon.

The Anasazi people first appeared in the region about 2,000 years ago and, after c.AD500, began to move from scattered villages into the densely populated cliff dwellings. By c.AD1200 their influence had spread throughout the southwest, but within a hundred years they had abandoned their canyon dwellings and disappeared.

After centuries of disuse, the Canyon de Chelly was re-occupied in the 18th century by the Navaho who moved in to the area from New Mexico.

Canyon de Chelly has been a refuge for thousands of years. The Anasazi people, or Basketmakers, first left their woven baskets in caves between c.2500 and c.2000BC. By AD450, they had begun to build houses under the protection of the cliffs – the beginning of a trend that would result in the monumental cliff dwellings.

At the head of the canyon, Chinl Wash, flanked by broad white sands, runs between brightly coloured sandstone cliffs some 30 feet (10m) high. As the canyon winds its way through the plateau, the cliffs rise higher and higher. Halfway through, where the tributary Monument Canyon joins,

the plateau rim is almost 1,000 feet (300m) above the canyon floor. Here the water of the wash is finally absorbed completely by the deep sand, except during periods of heavy summer thunderstorms when flash floods may rush the length of the canyon.

White House settlement was a small cluster of buildings created by the Anasazi during the Great Pueblo period (c. AD1050). It consists of two sections: one on the canyon floor built against the cliff face and the other high above in a rock shelter within the cliff itself. The two sites were originally connected by a four-story building. The lower structure had between 45 and 60 rooms and one kiva, or ceremonial chamber; the upper section had more than ten rooms. Rock paintings adorn the walls of the shelters. The later Navaho inhabitants placed burial cists within both ruins.

The earliest rock art here was created by the Pueblo builders, the Anasazi. Later paintings are the work of the Navaho.

Spider Rock (above) is the most dramatic geological feature of the canyon. It stands nearly 800 feet (245m) high.

During their early history at Canyon de Chelly, the Navaho had to oppose the troops of the Spanish and then the conquering Americans. Here two Navaho look across the wash of the canyon.

USA

o'N

Mexico
109°25'W

Mountains

Mountains are the points on Earth that are closest to the heavens, and in many cosmologies they are seen as the centre of the world, forming a link between earth and sky. A mountain summit is often a sacred place, where mortals may draw close to the spirit world.

Mount Fuji (above), Japan's most sacred peak. Members of the Fujiko sect claim it has a soul.

According to the Hebrew Scriptures, Moses spoke to God and received the Ten Commandments on the summit of Mount Sinai, a peak whose identity remains uncertain. It was on Mount Carmel that Elijah triumphed over the priests of Baal, on Mount Horeb that he heard the word of God, and from the Mount of Olives that Jesus ascended into heaven. Bear Butte, a high ridge in the plains of South Dakota, is regarded as sacred by local Native Americans and is used for vision quests (see pp.42–3) and other rituals.

Mountains are also seen as abodes of gods and goddesses, especially in those regions where the peaks are high enough to be veiled in clouds. According to the Pima people of California, a powerful deity, Siuhu ("Elder Brother"), lives at the end of a deep labyrinth in the mountains adjacent to Pima country; he acts as a protector and is responsible for rain, crops and tobacco.

In the Japanese Shinto religion, mountains such as Mount Fuji are not simply the dwellings of mountain deities but, according to some, their physical embodiments. The Navaho likewise view certain mountains as the bodies of their most important nature spirits: a male who

In this Hindu painting of c.1690 from Rajasthan, India, the god Krishna uses Mount Govardhana to shield villagers from a storm sent by the god Indra.

According to Genesis, *Noah's Ark came to rest on Mount Ararat in Turkey after the Flood.*

clouds as breath.

Hindus and Jains regard a golden mountain called Meru as the centre of the cosmos. The roots of Mount Meru are believed to be in the underworld, and the mountain is said to be wider at the top than the bottom, like an open lotus blossom. The abode of the gods, it is represented in Hindu temples as the roof-tower that surmounts the shrine.

As marking the centre of the world in many cultures (see pp.24–5), mountains are also seen as the symbolic ends of the Earth and sheltering the territory of the chosen people who live in their shadow. The protection offered may, however, be dependent on pilgrimage and sacrifice, such as that performed in the Aztec era by the citizens of Tenochtitlan, their mountain-ringed capital.

In north European folklore, mountains are often said to be the dwelling-places of kindly (but mischievous) dwarves expert in metalwork and in the forging of magic rings and swords.

rules all plants and wildlife, and a female in charge of water and water creatures. The male figure is believed to stretch along two mountain chains, the Chuska and Carrizo: his legs lie along the Carrizo, his neck at a mountain pass and his head at Chuska Peak. The female lies across the valley with her feet and body resting on various mesas and her head supported by Navaho Mountain. Some peoples see the rocks of a mountain as bones, the streams as blood, the vegetation as hair and the

TWISTED FACE

The Iroquois of eastern North America have a secret healing organization known as the False Face Society. During rituals, members wear carved wooden masks which represent the various Iroquois spirits who are believed to exist as disembodied faces in the forest. The origin of one spirit, Twisted Face, is said to have involved a dramatic encounter with a mountain. According to legend, Twisted Face was a giant who lived near the Rocky Mountains. One day he met up with the creator and argued that he, the giant, had made the Earth. In order to settle the argument the two decided to see who could move a mountain by magic. The giant called out to the mountain, and it moved slightly. Then the creator called out, and the mountain rushed toward him. As it approached, the giant turned around and it smashed him in the face, breaking his nose.

A mask representing the Iroquois spirit, Twisted Face.

Volcanoes and unearthly fires

The power of the Earth explodes into fierce and vivid reality when volcanoes erupt. It is difficult not to imagine the mythical fury of underworld beasts and the rage of gods as fire and ash surge into the sky in towering clouds, then rain destruction on the land below. The Greeks believed that the hundred-headed monster Typhon was subdued by the gods and chained to the land beneath Mount Etna and that, as the monster surged against its chains, it moved the earth and blasted the air with fire and smoke.

Volcanoes were sometimes viewed in a more positive light. In a myth of the Tsimshian people of British Columbia, the trickster spirit Raven brought light to humankind from a coastal volcano which remained active into the 18th century. However, even if volcanoes brought fire and light and, in the generations after an eruption, renewed fertility in the soil, their destructive impact guaranteed fear and respect. In Hawaii, sacrifices were thrown into the crater of Kilauea in order to ease the wrath of Pele, the goddess of volcanoes. The preferred gift was a suckling pig. People still throw offerings of food into the crater, and some witnesses claim to have seen Pele in the guise of an old woman before an eruption.

When a volcano is dormant or extinct, it continues to have the status of a supreme being. The flanks of the Nicaraguan volcano Ometepe are dotted with prehistoric stone images, graves and burial urns, all pointing to a belief in its supernatural power. Moreover, in a time-honoured ritual of reverence, thousands of pilgrims every year climb the high, snow-capped cone of the dormant volcano Mount Fuji, Japan's most sacred mountain.

Millions of years of erosion have stripped away the cones of some volcanoes to leave strange, gaunt lava cores soaring high above the land. These ancient, long-dead hulks continue to arouse a sense of mystery. Devil's Tower in Wyoming, venerated by native people, was the site chosen by Hollywood for the first alien spaceship to land in the Steven Spielberg movie *Close Encounters of the Third Kind*.

The Hawaian volcano, Mount Kilauea, associated with the goddess Pele.

MYSTERIOUS LIGHTS

During the great eruption of the Indonesian volcanic island of Krakatoa in 1883, the skies crackled with electricity and the masts and rigging of ships shimmered with the flames that sailors call St Elmo's fire. This strange electrical disturbance was at one time thought to be a visible sign of Castor and Pollux, the sons of Zeus associated with storms. Sailors in more recent times have claimed that the fire may be a harbinger of doom, akin to the ghost ship of the German Captain Falkenburg which is said to roam through northern seas with flames licking at its masthead. In fact, St Elmo's fire is a small electrical discharge caused by stormy weather.

Another mysterious light drifts through the still silence of marshes and hovers around graves. The aura of decay that pervades such places has led to the light being seen as the sign of a wandering spirit known as the will o' the wisp or jack o' lantern. In some places it is said to be the soul of a dead person, or an evil spirit luring the unwary traveller into a bog. Irish lore teaches that children who go outside after dark should wear their jackets inside out in order not to be ensnared by such a spirit.

The will o' the wisp is now known to be caused by the spontaneous combustion of gases rising from decaying vegetable matter.

The will o' the wisp, once thought to be an evil spirit.

Devil's Tower, a giant column of basaltic lava in Wyoming, was once the core of a volcano.

Vesuvius, Italy

Vesuvius, one of several volcanoes in southern Italy but the only active volcano on the European mainland, lies in a region of great seismic activity close to the point at which the Eurasian and African continental plates collide. The volcano began life under the waters of the Bay of Naples ten thousand years ago, and periods of activity over the millennia caused it to grow from an island of ash and pumice to a mountain some 6,000 feet (1,800m) high by the 1st century AD.

Near the foot of Vesuvius were the prosperous Roman towns of Pompeii, Herculaneum and Stabiae. On February 5, AD63, a severe earthquake destroyed much of Pompeii and other settlements. Then, for three days in AD79, Vesuvius erupted violently, burying Pompeii and Stabiae in ash and engulfing Herculaneum in a sea of volcanic mud. When the eruption ended, the upper part of the mountain collapsed.

The entire region around Vesuvius is volcanic. Naples, which lies less than ten miles (16km) to the west, is built on extinct craters and lies between Vesuvius and the Campi Flegrei (Phlegraean Fields), a cluster of nineteen active craters from which, according to the Roman poet Virgil (70BC–AD19), seeped the blood of giants defeated in battle by the gods. Virgil also claimed that Vesuvius lay on top of a giant called Alcyoneus. Numerous legends arose after the eruption of 79: for example, it was said that giants leapt through the smoke belching from Vesuvius and tore the mountain to pieces.

Mount Vesuvius, which appears as a dark patch in the centre of this aerial view (above), is part of a volcanic landscape stretching along the Bay of Naples and including the large volcanic island of Ischia.

Residents flee the eruption of Vesuvius in 1906. The volcano has a long history of activity that began toward the end of the last Ice Age.

A lava burst within the crater of Vesuvius. During the last great eruption of the volcano in 1944, rivers of lava transformed the towns of Massa and San Sebastiano into black, smoking lava fields.

A painting of the eruption of Vesuvius in 1870. The volcano had already erupted three times earlier in the 19th century, in 1822, 1838 and 1850. In 1872 the mountain exploded once again.

On the night of August 24, AD79, Vesuvius exploded and débris from the volcano engulfed the towns of Pompeii and Herculaneum. Pompeii was buried up to 25 feet (nearly 8m) deep in pumice and ash; Herculaneum was smothered by a flow of ash, lava and pumice that was in places more than 65 feet (nearly 20m) deep. In Pompeii, many people fled during the first two days of the eruption, when small lumps of pumice rained on the town. But the ash and poisonous fumes that struck the town on the third day caught the remaining citizens of Pompeii so suddenly that many suffocated. The ash solidified around bodies of the victims, preserving their final moments of life (above).

The crater of Vesuvius seen from across the Bay of Naples. The eruption of AD79 left the mountain several hundred feet lower than before.

Minerals, metals and precious stones

Iron pyrites

Feldspar

Quartz

The life of the rocks which formed the Earth ends when they are worn away by weathering and broken down into various sands and clays. Red ochre, one of the weathered compounds of iron, is a natural earth pigment that has been used for rock art ever since the first Paleolithic artists decorated the walls of their caves, as well as being a sacred substance used in rituals and for ceremonial body painting.

The Dinka people of the Nile basin region of the Sudan use mineral pigments for body painting.

Because metals, like human beings, were an earthly substance with spiritual potential (through smelting), they were listed in a cosmic hierarchy and associated with the seven known planets: lead was linked with Saturn, tin with Jupiter, iron with Mars, copper with Venus, mercury with Mercury, silver with the Moon, gold with the Sun.

Minerals and metals sometimes play a role in myths and folklore. For example, according to an Iroquois creation myth a mysterious stranger thrust a flint-tipped arrow into the ground and made the daughter of the first woman pregnant; the child to whom she gave birth was an evil trickster called Flint. In British folk belief it was traditionally thought that flint chippings were the tips of arrows shot by fairies.

Unusual mineral patterns in rock formations are often said to indicate sites where supernatural events took place. Earlier this century, some North American Ojibwa people were paddling down a river when they saw veins of white quartz snaking through a multi-coloured granite rock, and they took the pattern to mark the body of a spirit being. Other people in the region believed that shiny flat crystals of mica set with quartz and feldspar crystals in outcrops of pegmatite were the scales of the underwater manitou Mishipishew. Certain Australian Aboriginal groups believe that a sky god hurled crystals to the ground and that their sacred origin has given these rocks the power to assist shamans in finding lost souls. According to Buddhist belief, crystals are a symbol of spiritual knowledge. Throughout the West they are still the stock-in-trade of fortune tellers, deriving from an ancient interpretation of them as fragments of a star or of the throne of a god.

In antiquity analogies were sometimes made between the formation of metals and the creation of human life. Alchemists both in China and in western Europe thought that minerals grew in the body of the Earth like foetuses and that, given time, common metals would change into gold, the ultimate symbol of perfection.

Gold is remarkable because of its extraordinary lustre, durability, resistance to rust and the fact that it is malleable enough to be pounded into the thinnest leaf. It has always decorated the élites of the world, both during their lifetimes and after their deaths, and is

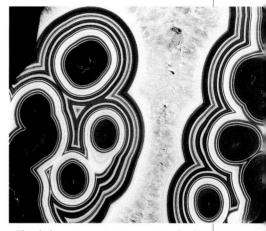

The whirling patterns in a cross-section of rock embody gigantic forces at work within the Earth.

almost universally regarded as a symbol of wisdom and immortality.

Iron was associated by Herodotus with "the hurt of man" and by the ancient Egyptians with the bones of the destructive god Seth.

SPIRITUAL STONES

Jewels are commonly regarded as symbols of the hidden treasures of knowledge or truth, and their shaping and cutting signifies the soul shedding itself of the physical body's corruption.

Individual jewels have acquired a variety of symbolic meanings. In Russian folk belief, the blood-red ruby was a cure for haemorrhages, and in Muslim lore a ruby supported the angel who held up the Earth. Emeralds were widely believed to cure many

Crystal, a solid penetrable by light, was seen by the ancients as magical and celestial.

ailments and were even alleged to have the power to calm stormy seas.

Hindus claim that the first sapphire was formed from one of Brahma's tears. According to a Hebrew legend, Aaron's Rod, which blossomed and bore fruit as a sign of Yahweh's power, was made of sapphire and engraved with ten letters representing the ten plagues that were sent to strike Egypt.

In Persia the diamond was once seen as a source of evil, whereas in other traditions its brilliance and hardness give it a spiritual significance.

Soil

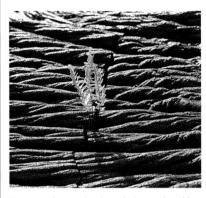

New growth struggles through the weathered lava crust of Mount Kilauea in Hawaii.

The soft body of the Earth holds the nutrients for almost all natural life. "Earth diver" origin stories, especially common among Native North American groups, draw attention to the soil's vitality. According to such myths, scraps of mud carried up from the bottom of the primordial sea by otters, ducks or other water creatures are magically transformed into the first dry land. The sacred role of the soil in the origins of life is also emphasized in accounts of the creation of human beings. Ancient Athenians believed that their original ancestor, Kekrops, was a half-man, half-serpent formed from the soil. Today, among the Aché of Paraguay, a newborn baby is placed on the soil to create a symbolic bond between the child and the sacred earth.

Certain deities celebrate the sustaining role of the soil in agriculture. According to Homer and Hesiod, Demeter was a goddess of the soil who made love to the hero Iasion in a ploughed field "in the fat land of Crete" and thereby produced the crops essential to survival.

The soil within a particular field may be regarded as having its own unique fertile essence. The Chuvashes, a Finno-Ugrian people, practise a fertility rite in which they "steal earth". This ritual is important because the spiritual potency, and hence the fertility, of soil is believed to vary from one cultivated field to another. An unsuccessful farmer might "steal" a clod of earth from a successful field to improve the land in his own field. The Chuvashes also believe that the "field mother", the sacred essence of the soil, can be transmitted from field to field on the hooves of a horse.

In Burma, soil is held in such high regard that it is taken to be one of the seven earthly metals, along with gold, silver, iron, copper, lead and tin.

Peat is an accumulation of semi-decayed plant material that has been dug for centuries as fuel.

The coming together of soil and rain, which is fundamental to fertility, is itself sacred to many agrarian peoples. Hopi mud dancers cover themselves with mud and charcoal for curing and rain-making rituals; the dancers may chase onlookers and smear them with mud in order to bring them into this celebration of life.

The deep spiritual importance of mud art may be appreciated in Mud Glyph Cave in Tennessee. Here, the visitor must wade and crawl through long, narrow passages in the dirt to reach an extraordinary complex of images that have been scraped and gouged out of the mud with fingers. The images, which include costumed figures and animals, among them some powerfully suggestive serpents and winged creatures, are believed to date from the 5th century AD, and to have been created by ancestors of the Cherokee or Creek peoples.

Ploughing is an age-old practice whose slow, seasonal rhythms have entered the collective unconscious of many agrarian peoples. Only after the wheeled ox-drawn plough had developed was the implement capable of breaking up the soils of northwest Europe, which are much harder and heavier than those of Mediterranean regions.

SOIL AND FERTILITY

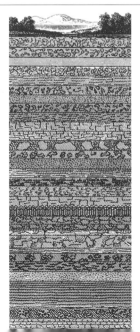

Soil, an essential component of the biosphere, is a life-sustaining substance of great complexity and fragility – a mixture of weathered minerals from rocks, partly decomposed organic detritus and countless living organisms that decompose organic detritus and recycle nutrients for plants.

Young soils, which have weathered relatively little, are rich in silicon, iron and aluminium. But in time rainwater dissolves and washes away minerals, and so soils become impoverished, even though their organic content, through the cycle of decay and renewal, may remain constant. Acid soils tend to lose minerals more readily than alkaline, which is why farmers add lime.

Erosion of the soil through loss of trees (which hold the soil together) and rainwater run-off can pose a threat to food supplies. Wind erosion also can be dramatic: scientists in Hawaii know when spring ploughing has started in China because the dust raised is carried right across the Pacific. Volcanoes enrich fertility by ejecting minerals that are eroded to become new, highly nutritious soil.

Trees and groves

In this sacred grove dedicated to the goddess Oshun in Oshogoo, Nigeria, a spirit figure has been carved into the bark of a tree. The oldest sanctuaries in the world were groves or woods. The Druids worshipped in groves of oak trees and their word for sanctuary was identical to that for grove or woodland glade. The tribes of the Volga also performed their religious ceremonies in sacred groves, each dominated by a central tree under which sacrifices were made.

Rooted firmly in the earth and reaching heavenwards with their branches, trees link the cosmos. With lifespans that often outlast those of human beings, they act as potent symbols redolent of time, maturity and endurance.

According to a post-medieval legend, the early Christian Joseph of Arimathea arrived at Glastonbury, England, in AD63, planted his staff in the ground on Wearyall Hill and watched it blossom into a hawthorn tree. Certainly there was a tree here, known as the Holy Thorn, that bloomed at Christmas, and although it was cut down by a Puritan in 1643 its descendants survived; in 1951 a new Holy Thorn was planted on the hill.

The annual cycle of deciduous trees, through budding, flowering, leaf-fall and the bearing of fruit, provides visible proof, on the largest scale, of the creative force within nature. Trees have therefore come to be seen as symbols of fertility. The Yarralin people of the

THE GREEN MAN

The Green Man is a nature spirit associated with the woodlands of Europe. His popularity was such that his image was carved in medieval churches. Known in England as Jack in the Green and in Russia and the Balkans as Green George, he is usually depicted wearing horns and wreathed in foliage. His ability to control the rains was recognized in Russia on St George's Day, when a man disguised as Green George was covered with branches and pushed into a stream in order to ensure summer rain.

The Green Man, a European fertility figure, seen here in a springtime ceremony in an early 19th-century English street.

Northern Territory of Australia have a Dreaming site for their *karu*, or uniniti-ated males, at a billabong near Lingara. The trees that grow around the site sup-posedly sprang from the semen of a group of *karu* who had stopped there; each of the trees is said to be an indi-vidual *karu*, and they are led by a large dead tree known as the "boss" *karu*. Men gather clay from the billabong and grind it with scrapings of bark to create a potion that they believe will attract women. Women also have Dreaming trees, some of them at sites where they can receive the spiritual seed necessary for birth.

Many of the gods and goddesses of ancient Greece were believed to inhabit sacred groves, to which people would retire for prayer or contemplation. The early Germanic peoples regarded oak groves as sacred, and would enter them to ask questions and listen for the answers in the rustling of the leaves. Today, many neo-pagans call their out-door meeting places "groves".

The Garden of Gethsemane, on the slope of the Mount of Olives, where Christ was arrested: gardens represent the taming of the forest.

THE SYMBOLISM OF FRUIT

Fruit has often been used symbolically to portray a state of paradisal bliss. Some fruits share the symbolic properties of the egg.

The vine is an ancient symbol of fecundity in various traditions, but in the Mediterranean lands it is also associated with sacrifice: it is the emblem of the Greek god Dionysus, who became linked with sacrifice under the influence of the cult of Orphism.

The pomegranate, with its many seeds in a juicy pulp, is a fertility symbol with overtones of love, marriage and the bearing of many children; it also suggests the oneness of the cosmos. One of the most positive of fruit symbols is the peach, which in the East is linked with immortality, longevity, youth and protective magic.

The acorn was sacred to the Scandinavian thunder god Thor, as part of a cult of the sacred oak tree.

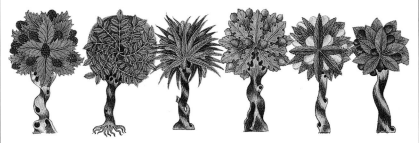

Delphi, Greece

Delphi lies beneath sheer cliffs on the rugged south-western slope of Mount Parnassus in mainland Greece. According to Homer, the god Apollo made the place his sanctuary after ridding it of a great serpent, Python. It is not known when the famous oracle was established, but from the 6th century BC Delphi with its shrine of Apollo became one of the most renowned sacred sites in Greece. A temple was built to the god and over the centuries a vast complex grew up around the site. However, the oracle remained Delphi's focal point. The Pythian priestess gave her cryptic messages from a chamber deep inside the temple which housed the *omphalos*, a carved stone said to be the centre of the world (see pp.25–6). It was believed that the priestess's prophecies were inspired by powerful, spiritual vapours which rose from a large crevice beneath the stone. After *c*.300BC the oracle began to lose its authority and in *c*.AD390 the Emperor Theodosius had the temple closed as anti-Christian.

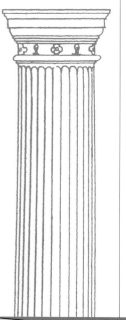

THEATRE

TEMPLE OF APOLLO

COLUMNS

160
120
80
40
0
ft

A theatre (above) was added to the complex at Delphi in the 4th century BC. Its seats rose in 35 tiers up a slope and could accommodate as many as 5,000 people.

Inside the temple, a plan of which can be seen above, stood statues of Zeus and Apollo; the sides of the building were filled with riches: four tripods of gold given by Tyrant of Syracuse and donations of sculptures of gods, heroes, horses, and goats.

The first temple at Delphi was destroyed by fire. It was rebuilt with the help of the king of Egypt, only to be destroyed by an earthquake some 200 years later. The final temple, the ruins of which still stand (above), was built in the 4th century BC and was supported by magnificent Doric columns.

Over the centuries, a large ceremonial and entertainment complex grew up around the temple. In the 2nd century BC, a stadium (above) for athletic contests, games and musical competitions was constructed. It was able to hold 7,000 people.

The Greek god Apollo (above), to whom the temple at Delphi was dedicated, killed the serpent which guarded the famous oracle. The act was believed to mark the triumph of the Olympian gods of light over the deities of darkness – but alternatively it has been interpreted as the final defeat of the Earth Goddess by a new patriarchal system of belief.

Visitors to the oracle washed in the Castalian Spring, then climbed the Sacred Way past the Treasury of the Athenians, shown here.

The Tree of Life

The tree is a powerful image of cosmic integration: it sends its roots down into the underworld, reaches its trunk upwards to the sky and spreads its branches in a leafy bower over all humanity. In many creation myths that feature multiple worlds or levels of existence, the tree stands solid as the single unifying feature, a conduit for the flow of divine energy. The image is found across a broad span of civilizations, and there are many variations on the theme. In some traditions it flourishes in paradise, or on a sacred mountain. At its roots a fountain of spiritual refreshment may gush. A serpent coiled around the base of the trunk may symbolize spiralling earth energy (or else destruction). Birds nesting in the topmost canopy may represent souls, or heavenly messages; fruits may signify the celestial bodies. Forming a network of communication, the tree was sometimes believed to offer a route to the first people who clambered up its trunk and up through its branches to the present world.

In Norse myth, the gods meet daily under Yggdrasil, the Tree of Life, shown here in a 19th-century image.

Cabbalistic and other occult traditions reverse the cosmic tree, depicting the roots nourished from the sky.

In Scandinavian mythology, the giant ash tree Yggdrasil unites the cosmos: it draws sacred water from springs and wells at its base and supports a host of supernatural beings in its branches. On the highest branch sits an eagle scanning the world for Odin, chief of the gods, who in a major episode of myth was to hang himself on the tree as a sacrifice in order to gain knowledge of the runic symbols used in divination. There is an analogy with Christ's sacrifice, and indeed medieval iconography often shows the Crucifixion on a tree rather than a cross. In many cultures, the tree is regarded not only as a symbol of cosmic unity, but also as the source of life. The Herero people of southern Africa believe that the first humans, as well as cattle, came from a tree called Omum-borombonga, in the grasslands south of the Kunene River. The tree is still alive, and when people pass it they leave offerings of small green twigs.

THE GODDESS IN THE TREE

Egyptian tomb paintings often depict the sacred tree above or beside a spring bubbling with the waters of life. A woman is sometimes shown embodied in the tree, her task being to provide food and drink for the inhabitants of the underworld.

The Yakut of Siberia also have a tree goddess. They relate how the first man, on setting out to explore the world, saw a giant tree which joined heaven, earth and the underworld and talked to the gods through its leaves. The youth was lonely, and so he asked the spirit of the tree to help him; a grave-eyed woman rose up from beneath the roots and offered him milk from her breasts. After the first man had drunk, he was filled with so much power and energy that no earthly thing could harm him.

According to the ancient Egyptians, a spirit-being known as a ba *emerged from the bodies of dead people. Here, a* ba *outside a tomb is fed and cared for by the Egyptian tree of life.*

DARWIN'S TREE OF LIFE

In his theory of natural selection, Charles Darwin (1809–82) laid down the basis of modern theories of the evolution of species. There is a famous analogy in *The Origin of the Species* in which Darwin compares living creatures to a great tree which he calls the Tree of Life. The green and budding twigs represent the existing species and the old wood represents fossils. As the tree grows, the living twigs branch out on all sides. Successful branches shade and kill the surrounding weaker offshoots, just as successful species and groups of species have overcome their competitors. Most of the young twigs drop off, although some remain as thin and straggly branches, representing the threatened species. A few twigs become great branches, and a small number become major limbs, which support a dense foliage of new twigs and leaves at the top of the tree.

According to Darwin, "As buds give rise by growth to fresh buds, and these, if vigorous, branch out and overtop on all sides many a feebler branch, so by generation I believe it has been with the great Tree of Life, which fills with its dead and broken branches the crust of the Earth and covers the surface with its ever-branching and beautiful ramifications."

Images and Structures

The natural landscape, as well as being our richest and readiest source of metaphor, has also carried on its surfaces, both above ground and underground, some of the most impressive and enigmatic artefacts that humankind has ever created.

Dotted around ancient stretches of terrain are monuments whose function continues to intrigue archaeologists and anthropologists: paintings accomplished far from daylight in the most inaccessible reaches of caves; avenues of rocks leading to massive henges; vast artificial mounds and hills; straight tracks in the desert plotted with the precision of a modern motorway but leading apparently nowhere; and countless others whose precise purpose may forever remain a mystery.

The Paleolithic animal paintings in the caves of Lascaux in France and Altamira give the lie to the commonplace notion that art progressed inevitably from primitivism to subtlety, through stages of increasing sophistication. These are images that speak to us directly but mysteriously, like many ancient artefacts, across vast tracts of time.

The rock paintings of the Dogon people of Mali in West Africa fill the landscape with rich symbolic meaning. In some cultures ancient rock art is interpreted as having a supernatural origin.

Early cave art

Prehistoric cave art, and particularly examples from sites in western Europe and Africa, provides us with some of humankind's most powerful animal imagery, suggesting a deeply felt relationship with the animal world which today is difficult for us even to imagine.

The cave paintings of western Europe (in particular southern France and northern Spain) from the Upper Paleolithic period, some of them as much as 30,000 years old, are justly renowned.

Sometimes prehistoric artists suggested the twists and turns of moving animals with complicated naturalistic perspectives which would not be seen again for thousands of years.

Decorated with beasts and abstract markings, those works mostly date to the last phase of the Ice Age ending about 10,000 years ago. A variety of techniques was used, from multicoloured painting in red, yellow and ochres (earth pigments), to blacks and violets from manganese oxides, to incised work in the cave walls.

Electric light, stairs and pavements now intrude on many Paleolithic cave sites, but for prehistoric peoples the caves were filled with absolute darkness, and often consisted of tortuous networks of passages. From a modern perspective it is hard to imagine that this underground landscape did not influence the artists' choice of what to create.

Rock paintings on the Tassili plateau in Algeria, c.4000BC or later. The cave art of the Sahara appeared after that of northwestern Spain and southwestern France, which rarely depicted human figures. The Algerian artists appear to have been early pastoralists rather than hunters.

In some of the shelters and caves the entrance areas are wide and dry, and served as living spaces. At Altamira in Spain and Le Poisson, La Madeleine and many other caves in France, there are rock paintings and engravings that were probably in close proximity to domestic life, as has been suggested by the discovery of the remains of hearths and animal bones and the débris of flint-knapping. Others, however, have been found at the end of deep passages which may wind far into the earth, as at Rouffignac in France, where a special train is now provided to enable modern visitors to see the site. Squeezing through subterranean mazes, the artists must have crouched in flickering light (there is evidence of stone bowls filled with animal fat, using wicks of grass, lichens and juniper) to create their works.

Few human beings and no objects were depicted. Most of the imagery shows animals, and the frequency of mammoths, bison, reindeer and other beasts of the hunt is consistent with the view that the cave art was motivated by "sympathetic magic", conducted to ensure hunting success. However, other interpreters associate the cave sites with fertility, and in the popular imagination the underground darkness of these womb-like places may be thought to reinforce this idea. Some anthropomorphic figures found among the animals

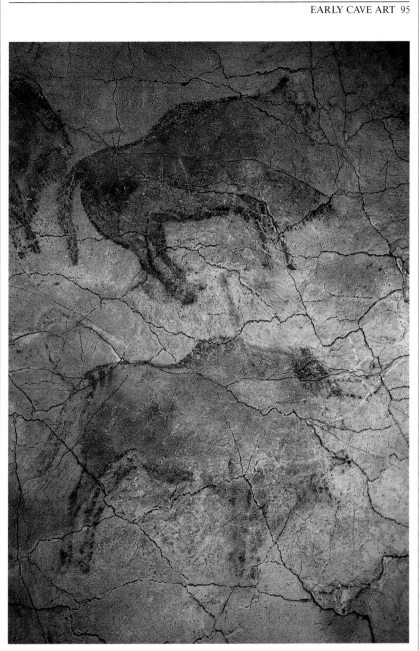

Part of the magnificent painted ceiling of the cave at Altamira near Santander in northern Spain, discovered in 1879. It is decorated with ochre paintings of bison and other animals.

Prehistoric rock paintings of animals and humans in a cave in the Matopo Hills, Zimbabwe.

have been seen as spirit guardians, comparable to the shamans of later cultures. However, there is no conclusive evidence that the caves were ever put to ritual use.

Most of the animals depicted by Paleolithic artists can be identified as

A deer in the caves at Altamira in Spain, painted during the Magdalenian period (c.13000BC).

species now extinct, such as the mammoth, or immediately recognized as the ancestors of modern animals, such as the elk and deer. However, in a small recess of the cave of Les Trois Frères in southwestern France resides a creature that seems to have the feet and legs of a human and the torso, arms and tail of an animal; the head is indistinct. The Abbé Breuil, a French archaeologist who worked during the early and middle part of this century, imagined and recorded this figure as a medicine man or "sorcerer", clothed in an animal skin and wearing a ceremonial headdress of animal horns.

Other scholars of the time associated the image with hunting magic, seeing it as a magician or spirit who controlled animals. The interpretation of this figure, with its human and animal attributes, remains controversial.

Some experts perceive in the cave art sites a symbolic landscape of imagery in which various galleries and passageways associated with different subjects are arranged in such a way as to convey fundamental ideas about life and nature. Sites such as Lascaux (see pp.98–9), with its Hall of the Bulls and Chamber of Felines, perhaps make this theory attractive, but unfortunately the mythologist Joseph Campbell's words are likely to remain true for the foreseeable future: "to the mystical function that each of these galleries served – for millennia – we have no clue".

It is generally assumed that the cave painters were male, but there is also a theory that the early interpreters of cave art underplayed the number of female, vulvic images, and in the process concealed some work that had been done by women. Various line markings have been read as records of menstruation, although the earlier hypothesis that they are calendrical is still plausible.

AFRICAN CAVE AND ROCK ART

Neolithic rock and cave art in Africa gives us vital evidence for the domestication of animals, and for the adaptation of wildlife to climatic change. Surprisingly, the African rock art sites were discovered by Westerners before the European sites came to light.

Initially, only wild animals were shown. The North African buffalo (*Bubulus antiquus*), which appears in rock engravings of the period from *c*.7000BC to *c*.4500BC, may be a lord of animals responsible for the movements of wild herds of various species of interest to human hunters; it makes a suggestive parallel with Lascaux's bison. Other wild beasts depicted include the elephant, rhinoceros, hippotamous, giraffe, ostrich and antelope.

From about 8,000 years before the present, domestication appears with increasing frequency. Pastoral scenes, with herds of cattle, sheep, asses and goats, form a dramatic contrast with the wild beasts of the more familiar European Paleolithic paintings. Later, horses appear (first with chariots, then with riders), and finally camels. Various Saharan sites show attempts to domesticate beasts such as the giraffe.

In the Tassili region of the Sahara (see p.94), more than 15,000 examples of rock art are known, including a group of paintings, from *c*.6000BC, characterized by stylized human figures with rounded featureless heads.

Cave paintings by the Dogon people of Mali depicting the creation of the world by the god Amma, and Nommos (supernatural creator beings) falling from heaven to earth.

The wealth of cave art in southern Africa includes, in the Makumbe Cave, Zimbabwe, a superb painting produced accretively during a period from almost two thousand to a few hundred years ago, in a range of styles, depicting two large elephants, humans, a rhinoceros and antelopes. The technique of superimposing images at different times, also found in Europe, supports the idea that the motivation was ritualistic rather than aesthetic.

Lascaux, southwest France

The complex of caves at Lascaux in the Dordogne, southwestern France, contains one of the most extraordinary displays of prehistoric rock art. On their discovery in 1940 the high artistic quality of the paintings and engravings – which had probably been undisturbed for 17,000 years – was immediately evident. Less obvious was why apparently several generations of artists had adorned the caves with many hundreds of representations of animals.

The Lascaux artists often worked close to the cave roof (a feat impossible without scaffolding or ladders) to produce paintings which were very difficult to view from the cave floor, especially by the pale light of the artists' tallow lamps (hundreds of these have been found in the caves). The presence of such inaccessible art implies that the paintings were not merely decorative, and the most widely held view is that they were linked with hunting. Most of the pictures are of large game mammals, such as bison, aurochs (an extinct bovine), horse and deer, and some animals are depicted with wounds. It has been proposed that the paintings are "trophy arrays" of notable hunting successes. Another theory is that the artists were involved in a form of "sympathetic magic", supposedly drawing a beast to its death in the hunt by fixing its image and gaining control over its soul. The cave, it has been suggested, may have been the site of rites conducted by a shamanistic "master of animals".

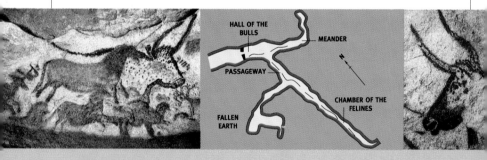

Another artist probably painted the black-headed horse (above) some time after the large aurochs was drawn. The artist has taken great care to place the horse in harmony with the larger animal.

The "Rotunda" or "Hall of Bulls" provides a dramatic entrance to the cave, its walls covered with giant outlines of aurochs and many smaller animals. The next chamber, the "Axial Gallery", is decorated with brightly painted animals, their colours enhanced by the white calcite on the walls. Beyond the Nave, the chamber narrows until it opens into a gallery filled with images, including several engraved felines.

The head of an aurochs, outlned in a manganese oxide pigment, forms part of a painting which measures 18 feet (5.5m) long.

HALL OF THE BULLS

MEANDER

PASSAGEWAY

CHAMBER OF THE FELINES

FALLEN EARTH

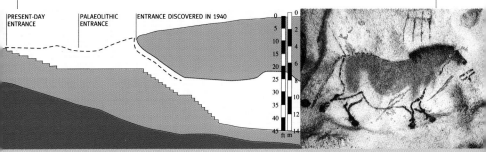

Aurochs, horses and other animals decorate the north wall of the Rotunda, facing the Axial gallery.

PRESENT-DAY
ENTRANCE

PALAEOLITHIC
ENTRANCE

ENTRANCE DISCOVERED IN 1940

0
5
10
15
20
25
30
35
40
45
ft

0
2
4
6
8
10
12
14
m

In September 1940 four boys from Montignac explored a dark hole they had found in the hillside. Using a crude lamp to light their way, they scrambled down the steep slope of debris into a large open chamber. The open space engulfed the light, but when they passed through a narrow archway into another,

lower chamber, the lamp lit the bright reds, yellows and blacks of a mass of painted animals on the ceiling. The slope they had come down was not the original entrance to the cave, but a crack in the roof: the Paleolithic entrance had long since collapsed and entombed the images within.

One of the so-called "Chinese horses" of Lascaux (above), outlined in black in a style resembling that of later Chinese artists.

ATLANTIC OCEAN

Germany

FRANCE

Austria

44°N

Portugal Spain

Italy

1°30'E

Images on rock

Ancient open-air rock art sites form part of the sacred landscape of many Aboriginal groups and are important in their mythology, for the spirits said to inhabit such sites and for the supernatural events that are believed to have taken place there in the past. For example, in the Western Kimberley mountains of northwestern Australia, the local Aborigines explain the existence at some sites of several layers of super-imposed art as the work of tricksters who deliberately defaced sacred caves by drawing over the paintings left by the heroic ancestors of the Dreaming (see pp.34–5). Rock paintings may also mark territorial boundaries and the sites of significant real events (such as a particularly fruitful hunt), or they may be associated with powerful individuals: this may help to explain the presence of human handprint "signatures" at caves in Queensland.

Many of the rock art traditions have been lost: we have the evidence itself, but no means of interpreting it. However, some practices remain alive: for example, in the 1930s an archaeologist investigating a shelter in Western Australia found freshly painted images of a dugong or sea cow, a freshwater tortoise, and the liver of a stingray. Throughout Australia paintings are occasionally retouched or renewed, sometimes as part of rituals intended to increase the numbers of kangaroos, alligators, yams and other sources of food (see p.103).

Some of the most remarkable rock art is found in south-central and southern Africa, produced over many centuries by the Bushmen (San) who were the region's principal human inhabitants before the migration of Bantu peoples after c.1600 confined them largely to the Kalahari and Namib deserts. The greatest concentration of San art is found in the Drakensberg mountains of the eastern Cape, an area from which the San were pushed at around the end of the 19th century by both the Bantu and European settlers between whom they found themselves sandwiched. (San artists of this late

Mythical beings and animals depicted on a rock near Peterborough, Ontario, probably by Algonkian artists. Among the creatures represented are game animals such as caribou, rabbits and deer, and anthropomorphic beings. The identities of such beings, like the original purpose of the petroglyphs, is difficult to determine. However, one figure with rabbit's ears depicted at Lake Mazinaw may be Nanabozho, a trickster of Algonkian mythology otherwise known as Great Hare.

Two elands and a giraffe are among the animals painted on a rock face in the Tsodilo Hills of northeastern Botswana by San artists.

lope. Some paintings depict ceremonies which appear to represent an individual's transformation into an eland being. The painted rituals resemble, in form at least, practices still current among the San.

The Bantu peoples who had displaced the San in most of southern Africa by *c*.1800 left their own legacy of rock paintings (much of it formerly attributed to the San by European scholars on the grounds that they were the only people of the region still producing rock art). Bantu art, centred on Zimbabwe, reflects a culture that practised the sacrifice of infirm kings in order to ensure the continued prosperity of the land.

period depicted scenes of cattle rustling from the herds of both groups of newcomers.) The Drakensberg art includes engraved animals on stone and also painted images reflecting San mythology and belief, such as their reverence for the eland, the largest species of ante-

A PAINTER AT WORK

Kakadu National Park, in the Alligator River region of northern Australia, has thousands of rock paintings spanning several millennia. Some of the most striking were made this century by Najombolmi, a man who owned lands of the Bardmardi clan on Deaf Adder Creek. He worked for European hunters at buffalo hunting camps but also spent time travelling in the bush, painting. In the year before his death he became concerned with the decline of traditional beliefs and the abandonment of the land, and travelled to a site at Anbangbang which had paintings of two men and their wives. Najombolmi repainted the men and women and expanded the scene into two family groups. He added three characters from the Dreaming story of creation: Namargon, the Lightning Man, Bargini, his wife, and Namondjolk, an evil spirit.

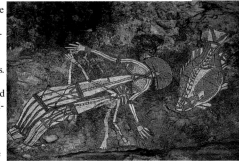

A rock painting from Kakadu National Park, Arnhem Land. It depicts mythical beings from the Dreaming (see pp.34–5).

Rock art rituals

The San (Bushmen) dance through the night to attain an ecstatic trance-like state through which they contact the creative spirit energy called ntum.˙ *Their dance is depicted in sacred painted rock shelters.*

When artists paint the surface of a rocky outcrop, they are imposing cultural expression on the ancient body of the Earth. It is widely believed that this conjunction of the human and natural worlds creates a source of great power and spiritual energy.

Rock art sites sometimes function almost like temples in drawing people together in worship. During the later 17th century, when Native North Americans still conducted their ancient rituals in the open, the French priests Dollier de Casson and De Brehant de Galinée came upon a strange, human-shaped rock near Lake Erie that had been embellished with red ochre and facial features. In the area were many camps of people who had stopped to pay their respects to the stone and to leave offerings of skins and provisions in the hope of ensuring their safe passage across the often treacherous waters of Lake Erie and Lake Huron. Belief in the power of such sites continues. For example, in northern Canada, the Ojibwa people still believe that a certain lakeside rock painting site is the haunt of spirits; the Ojibwa either leave offerings of tobacco there or will travel quickly past on the opposite side of the lake.

These sacred places are also sources of inspiration for shamans who seek to acquire knowledge from the spirit world through dreams and visions. A broad shelf of rock high on a granite cliff in the region of the Great Lakes, a neighbouring gloomy, cave-like crevice and other

"INCREASE ROCKS"

Australian Aboriginals believe that some rocks and rock paintings possess the power to increase the supply of game animals, plants and other essential food sources. In the Western Kimberleys, Aboriginals sometimes rub with their hands standing stones associated with beings from the Dreaming, in the belief that the dust that is thereby created will bring forth new life.

When Aboriginals in the Oenpelli region of western Arnhem Land want to increase the supply of water-snakes, they beat a rock painting of a water-snake with a bough to flush out its

"Jabiru Dreaming", a sacred rock in Northern Territory.

spirits, then tell the spirits to go to waterholes and become large snakes. At a site near South Alligator River, Aboriginals build fires under the painting of a yam in the belief that the smoke will pick up the spirits of the plant and spread them over the land.

The waters of Lake Superior at sunset. The rocks around the Great Lakes play an important part in the beliefs of the local Algonkian peoples.

sites nearby have all been painted with the figures of animals and humans that appear to have been inspired by a dream or vision.

In southern Africa, the San or Bushmen of the Kalahari (see pp. 100–101) painted rocks with scenes of medicine men in rituals, sometimes dancing into an ecstatic state in order to gain supernatural power. According to the San, many of the complicated abstract patterns also found on the rocks were painted by shamans; recent research has demonstrated that the designs are similar to the neurological patterns that are produced in a state of trance.

Some people, such as the Tukano of South America, use similar patterns as the basis for their decorative art, and particular configurations are owned by different groups.

Images out of the earth

When the Oglala Sioux of the North American Plains conduct a sweatlodge ritual (see pp.40–41), earth is removed from the centre of the lodge to make a pit where the hot stones are placed. The excavated earth is used to make a sacred path with a small mound at one end called *unci*, or "grandmother", a symbol of the Earth. When the ritual is over, the sacred ground is abandoned to the elements. Similarly, the intricate, painstakingly prepared sandpaintings used in Navaho curing rituals (see p.11) are simply swept away after use.

In Australia, ground sculptures are made as part of mortuary or healing

The Long Man of Wilmington in southern England a figure created out of a paving of white bricks which was placed there in 1874.

rituals. Among the Yolngu people of northeast Arnhem Land, members of the Liyagawumirri clan design a map which shows the springs and wells believed to have been made by the Djanggawul sisters, ancestral heroines from the Dreaming (see pp. 34–5). The sculpture is used as a grave and as a place to dispose of spiritually polluted food (that is, any food belonging to those close to the deceased).

Images may also be made by incising marks into the topsoil or vegetation to reveal a different coloration below. The White Horse of Uffington and other hill figures of England were made by removing the turf from chalklands to expose the underlying white chalk (see p.109), and it is known that a similar method was also practised in North America, although no images survive.

Turf mazes are a typically English form of incised earth imagery, although there are fascinating parallels with other cultures. Probably the oldest of the eight extant examples is the Walls of Troy maze near Brandsby, in Yorkshire, which is still tended to keep its outline sharp. The turf mazes are unicursal (that is, there is only one route through them, a single, winding path leading to the centre). More complex in form is an example at Alkborough, Lincolnshire, on a hill above the Humber valley. Probably cut in the 13th century by monks from Spalding Abbey, the maze is known as Julian's Bower, a reference to the tradition whereby Aeneas' son Julius supposedly brought mazes to the West. Based on twelve concentric circles, the design resembles the 12th-century maze on the floor of Chartres Cathedral, France.

Interpretations of the function of turf mazes concentrate on their uses for various dancing and walking rituals, linked with spring fertility rites. It is possible that the sudden changes of direction required by the convoluted route are associated with dizzying changes in consciousness, akin to the effect of hallucinogens, or at a more mundane level the exhileration of dance.

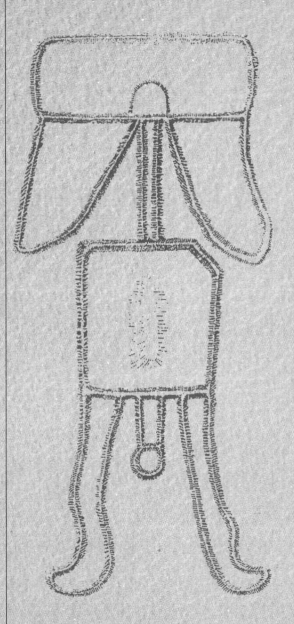

SAND SCULPTURE RITUAL

Ground sculptures are a common feature of rituals in Arnhem Land in Australia's Northern Territory. In *larrakan*, the final burial rite of the Gidjingali people, the dry bones of the deceased – who would have died years earlier – are packed into a decorated hollow log coffin and interred within a ground sculpture at the site of the grave. The coffin is buried in the stomach area of an image nearly 33 feet (10m) long of a sacred totemic being or *wongarr* called Ngarapia. He is said to have been a violent, dangerous man who was ultimately cornered by a group of warriors and run through with a stone-tipped spear. After death he was supposedly transformed into a large black rock, which can still be seen in the shallows surrounding the island of Burdja, off Cape Stewart; a hole in the rock which allows water to spurt through is thought to be the fatal wound.

The sand sculpture of Ngarapia is created during a dupun ceremony on the morning of the day on which the deceased is buried. The bones are crushed in order to fit inside the coffin.

Silbury Hill, southern England

Silbury Hill is a massive Neolithic man-made mound which rises just over 130 feet (40m) above the valley floor of the River Kennet in the chalklands of Wiltshire, southern England. It has long aroused both respect and curiosity: an important Roman road detoured around it, and the antiquarian John Aubrey wrote in 1663, when he conducted King Charles II on a tour of nearby Avebury, that "his Majesty cast his eie on Silsbury-hill about a mile off; which they had the curiosity to see, and walkt up to the top of it".

According to local legend, the hill was the tomb of an ancient king, Sil, buried with his horse. In 1723 an excavation at the summit uncovered bones, deer horns, an iron knife and a horse's bridle. The possibility of finding treasure buried deep in the mound prompted further excavations: in 1776 the Duke of Northumberland had a vertical shaft dug down to the original ground surface, and in 1849 one John Merewether tunnelled into the mound. They found neither tomb nor treasure.

The latest effort to solve the mystery of Silbury Hill was in 1967–8, when a team re-excavated Merewether's tunnel. The excavations showed that the builders of the hill began work *c*.2660BC, but why the mound was built still remained a mystery. Some authorities believe that it was raised to honour a chieftain; others see it as the womb of a pregnant mother goddess or as an *omphalos* marking the centre of the world.

SIX TIERS OF CHALK RETAINING WALLS — INFILL — AVEE

INNER MOUND

51°27'N
ATLANTIC OCEAN
UK
Germany   Poland
France   Austria
1°51'W   Italy

The smooth conical form of Silbury Hill (above) conceals the stepped layers that make up the inner core of the mound (above right). Silbury was built in three stages. First, a low mound was constructed. This was later enlarged using chalk blocks in sloped steps, held together with interlinking walls. Thirdly, the first two mounds were enclosed within a larger, stepped mound, built of chalk blocks in a honeycomb arrangement infilled with chalk rubble; the structure was then clad with soil and turf. It was once described as "a sort of snail with a flat shell, slender and having three or four entire turns"

A similar type of monument appeared at around the same time (c.2600BC) in ancient Egypt, when Zoser, a king of the Third Dynasty, ordered the construction of a tomb at Saqqara which took the form of a stepped pyramid.

The many mounds and monuments of the ancient kingdom of Wessex in southern England, including Silbury Hill, have been part of the working agricultural landscape for thousands of years.

As the map (above) and the aerial photograph (above right) show, Silbury Hill lies close to the great henge of Avebury (see pp.120–21). Many people believe that the two monuments must have been in some way related: for example, it has been suggested that the mound was used as a signal tower or beacon to summon people to rituals at Avebury. Many of the standing stones at Avebury have been destroyed for religious, superstitious or agricultural reasons, but the bulk of Silbury has resisted all but the shovels of archaeologists and treasure seekers. The sight of the strange, conical mound rising above the surrounding countryside continues to inspire and intrigue.

An engraving by the English antiquarian William Stukeley (1687–1765), who in the 1720s carried out the first serious archaeological investigations into Silbury, Avebury and other monuments. His theory, that they were associated with the Druidic rituals of the ancient Britons, was accepted for well over a century.

Images for the gods

Images created on the surface of the Earth may be so large that they cannot be seen in their entirety from ground level. Some of the most remarkable examples of such designs are to be found on the Nazca pampa, a desert plateau in the foothills of the Peruvian Andes. The brown-black, oxidized desert surface was scraped away to uncover the lighter subsoil – much in the same way that images were cut into the chalk downs of southern England – and form long narrow lines or tracks. The "artists" also created giant images of geometric

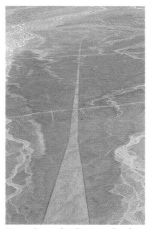

Nazca lines often begin and end in empty desert, prompting the theory that they were used for ritual walks.

This Nazca outline resembles a fox, an animal which, in Andean mythology, assisted the gods.

forms, such as triangles and spirals, together with outlines of monkeys, frigate birds, spiders and other creatures. These great earth drawings, discernible only from the air, were probably made by the Nazca people, whose culture flourished c.AD1–650. The size of the images has attracted much attention and has prompted various theories as to their purpose, ranging from the proposition that they are associated with Nazca astronomical or calendrical systems (unlikely in view of the fact that few astronomical alignments have been found) to the more fantastic suggestion that they were intended as navigation beacons for alien landing craft. The truth may be related to both these ideas: perhaps the designs were intended to be seen only by the deities believed to dwell in the heavens.

There is some evidence that the Nazca lines, in the distant past, were ritually swept. Our interpretation of this is perhaps illuminated by the observations of the anthropologist Gary Urton, who records seeing an Andean ceremony in which the plaza outside a village church was swept in strips, each strip belonging to a kinship group in the community; after the sweeping a statue of the saint to whom the church was dedicated was brought out and exhibited in a parade.

The Inca, who established an empire in the 15th century stretching from Ecuador to Chile known as the Land of the Four Quarters, built long straight roads, parts of which incorporated the older Nazca lines. The roads intersected

HILL FIGURES OF ENGLAND

At several places in the downlands of southern England ancient sculptors created striking images by cutting away the thin layer of grassy turf to reveal the white chalk beneath. One of the finest of these chalk figures is on Whitehorse Hill at Uffington in Oxfordshire, where the turf was cut away to create a great horse 374 ft (114m) long. It is not known who made the figure, which was once attributed to King Alfred the Great of Wessex (AD849–99), who was born at nearby Wantage. The animal resembles the stylized horse images on British coins of the period immediately preceding the Roman invasion, but it may be even older. It lies in an area which contains numerous significant prehistoric monuments: an ancient track, the Ridgeway,

One local folk myth claims that the White Horse at Uffington commemorates St George's victory over the dragon at nearby Dragon Hill. However, it is almost certainly prehistoric in origin.

passes nearby and the horse is close to Wayland's Smithy, a great standing stone. The horse has survived (and possibly changed in form) through the periodic removal of grass and weeds.

The identity of another famous chalk effigy, the 260ft (80m) tall giant near Cerne Abbas in Dorset, is also uncertain. The figure has a large erect penis and wields a club. In local tradition he is linked with fertility: May Day dances were once held on the hilltop above his head (see also p.106).

---

at the Inca capital of Cuzco ("Navel"), the street plan of which took the form of a giant jaguar or other feline, an animal which played a central role in Andean myth.

The deserts of the American southwest also furnished a massive canvas for ancient artists. Near Blyth in California several giant human figures and an animal were scraped out of the gravel terrace west of the Colorado River. The origin of these images is unknown, but one figure in Arizona resembles Hâ-âk, a monster in the creation mythology of the Pima people.

Some of the many burial mounds found in Wisconsin, Michigan and Iowa take the form of great effigies of human beings, birds, reptiles and other animals. One group of nine hundred mounds recorded at Harper's Ferry, Iowa, in the 19th century, included effigies of more than a hundred animals and around seventy birds, as well as many forms which were unidentifiable owing to erosion.

When the land in which these mounds stood came under cultivation, all but the most remarkable effigies were destroyed.

The Serpent Mound, Ohio

The Serpent Mound is one of the most striking and mysterious of all Native American monuments. It was constructed more than 2,000 years ago by people of the Adena or Hopewell cultures from yellow clay on a base of clay and stones.

One quarter of a mile (nearly 0.5km) long and built in the form of a snake with an egg in its mouth, the mound stands on a narrow promontory in the fork of Brush Creek and a smaller tributary in Adams County. Steep wooded slopes on one side and a sheer cliff 160 feet (50m) high on the other make the promontory itself an impressive sight, dominating the landscape.

The antiquarian Stephen D. Peet was among the first to propose that the mound was the effigy of a deity. In 1890 Peet wrote that "the shape of the cliff would easily suggest the idea of a massive serpent, and this with the inaccessibility of the spot would produce a peculiar feeling of awe, as if it were a great Manitou [divine spirit] which resided there". In Native American mythology the divinity known as Horned Serpent, Antlered Serpent or Water Monster is the guardian of sources of life arising out of the earth, especially water. The promontory overlooks an entire water catchment area, and the "egg" originally contained a small circle of burnt stones. A fire lit there would have been visible for miles and may have been intended as a sign that the serpent spirit of the waters was active and watchful.

The Serpent Mound was first interpreted by E.G. Squier and E.H. Davis in 1848 as part of the Smithsonian Institution's survey of ancient monuments in the Mississippi Valley. The researchers interpreted the serpent as a universal sacred symbol, used by Egyptians, Assyrians, Celts, Hindus and other peoples, and speculated about Old World influences in the building of the mound.

Snakes and serpents are powerful supernatural beings in many Native American mythologies. In the southwest, their images are engraved or painted on desert rocks, woven into blankets, painted on pottery or depicted in sandpaintings, such as this Navaho sandpainting of horned snakes.

The earthwork, which appears to represent an uncoiling snake, is more than 1,250 feet (380m) long.

By 1886 the mound, already damaged by treasure-hunters, sightseers and the effects of soil erosion, seemed destined to be turned into a cornfield. But P.W. Putnam of the Peabody Museum at Harvard University restored it, and from 1900 visitors were able to see the serpent effigy from a viewing tower (above).

Squier and Davis published their survey of the Serpent Mound in Ancient Monuments of the Mississippi Valley (1848), their groundbreaking study of prehistoric Native American sites from which this engraving is taken. The mound is one of hundreds of earthworks and burial mounds, many in the form of birds and animals, that were built in the region by people of the ancient Adena or Hopewell cultures.

Boulder effigies and medicine wheels

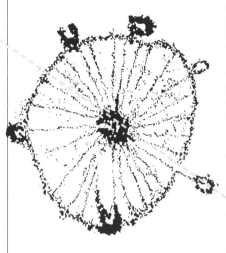

The Native American builders of the Big Horn "medicine wheel" (above) were probably of the Crow, Cheyenne, Shoshone or Arapaho peoples, all of whom hunted in the area.

On many high, remote hills in the northern plains and prairies of North America, rocks and boulders deposited by glaciers were arranged by prehistoric artists into geometric patterns or the outlines of human beings and animals. Even where they have not been disturbed or destroyed by farmers, the precise age and origin of the stone images are difficult to determine, but oral traditions record the legendary or mythical events behind their construction. For example, on a high knoll near Punished Woman's Lake in South Dakota, early European settlers discovered the larger than life-size stone effigies of a man and a woman, together with an unidentified figure, a number of cairns and some shallow pits. When the local Sioux were asked about the history of the effigies, they explained that the two figures were a woman who had run away from the husband she was forced to marry, and the man who was her first love. The monument was said to mark the spot at which the lovers were slain by the jealous husband.

The Sioux told a secular legend to account for the origin of the Punished Woman effigies (which were destroyed by 1914). However, the discovery elsewhere of numerous outlines of snakes and turtles (see opposite, below), creatures that feature prominently in traditional Native American religion, suggests that the boulder forms may in fact have been sacred in origin and purpose.

On high land in the northern plains, the stones sometimes form giant circles, often with massive cairns at their centres and rows of stones leading out to the edges like the spokes of wheels. No one knows why these effigies, known as "medicine wheels", were built, but some appear to have been used in rituals associated with astronomical events. Near the summit of Medicine Mountain, one of the highest peaks in the Big Horn Mountains of Wyoming, the "wheel" has 28 "spokes" and is almost 100 feet (30m) in diameter. There are six small cairns around the circumference of the circle. The form of this medicine wheel closely resembles the design of a Cheyenne sun dance lodge, a round building with a central post and 28 rafters. The lodge was reserved for sacred rituals connected with the sun, and it is possible that the medicine wheel was constructed with a similar purpose. It certainly appears to have some link with the solar cycle: one prominent cairn and the centre of the wheel are aligned with the position of the sun at dawn on the summer solstice.

A modern form of medicine wheel has arisen in recent years from a complex mix of Native American spirituality and Oriental mysticism. Among groups such as Sun Bear's Bear Tribe Medicine Society, the wheel has become a mandala, a symbol used by Buddhists to aid meditation. The participants in this 20th-century medicine wheel ritual gather 36 stones, each standing for a part of the universe, and create a huge circle representing the cosmos. The leader of the group, Sun Bear, places the skull of a sacred animal in the centre of the wheel as a symbol of the creator spirit, from whom all life radiates.

The Bulgarian artist Christo (born 1935) created a modern version of the boulder sculpture by painting these rocks in blues, mauves and pinks, altering their colour rather than their positions to create a striking landmark in the Morocco desert. Christo has used various man-made materials to create his temporary "environmental sculptures".

DESPERATE PATHS

Two boulder designs several hundred of miles apart are associated with similar legends of the death of a warrior. Near Cluny in Alberta a human figure lies part of the way along a line of boulders linking two cairns. It is said to mark a battle which took place in 1872 between the North Blackfoot and Blood peoples. In the 1960s, a Blackfoot elder identified the figure as that of Young Medicine Man, a Blood, who was killed by Walking With A Scalp, a Blackfoot. The

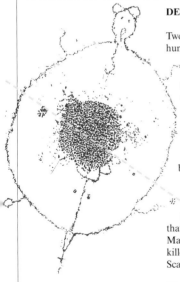

The boulder effigy of a turtle from Manitoba.

cairns allegedly mark where the duel began and ended, and the boulders indicate the course of the warriors. The effigy is on the spot where Young Medicine Man fell.

The top of Snake Butte in South Dakota has a similar grouping of cairns, effigy and boulder path. The site is known locally as the place where a Sioux warrior wounded an Arikara enemy who fled and eventually fell dead. The cairns are said to denote the place of the encounter and of the warrior's death, and the boulders represent his drops of blood. Near this construction, which is about half a mile (800m) long, the image of a turtle is said to represent the sacred animal symbol of the victor.

Moose Mountain, Saskatchewan

Like most of the "medicine wheels" made from rocks and boulders by prehistoric peoples on the northern plains of the United States and Canada (see pp.112–13), the large stone outline on Moose Mountain, Saskatchewan, resembles a drawing of the sun, with rays or "spokes" radiating from a central cairn. The original purpose of this and similar structures is difficult to determine. Some of them are very ancient: excavation at the Majorville Cairn in southern Alberta shows that the site was used at least 4,500 years ago. According to some estimates, the Moose Mountain medicine wheel site may be around 2,000 years old.

The Moose Mountain site presents one remarkable parallel with the Big Horn medicine wheel in Wyoming (see opposite, below, and p.112), a structure which, according to one theory, may have been constructed as a giant calendar of celestial events. Like Big Horn, the Moose Mountain wheel has one "spoke" slightly longer than the others and apparently aligned with the point on the horizon at which the midsummer sun rises. If this alignment was deliberate, then we can fairly assume that the other "spokes" at Moose Mountain were also aligned with heavenly bodies; but this cannot be determined with ease, because the trajectories of more distant stars in relation to the Earth have shifted considerably over several centuries. However, it is not unlikely that the alignments were originally linked to particularly bright stars or planets.

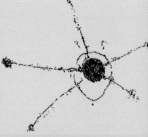

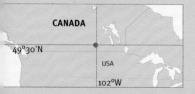

At Moose Mountain (above and above right), five "spokes", varying from 50 feet to 100 feet (15–30m) in length, radiate from a great

cairn at the centre of the wheel. Each line ends in a smaller cairn measuring 3 feet to 6 feet (1–2m) across. Although the surviving oral traditions of the Plains peoples provide little evidence of actual astronomical reckoning, the

alignment evidence from Moose Mountain, Big Horn and other medicine wheels suggests that the movements of stars and planets played a significant role in ancient Native American religion.

CANADA

49°30'N

USA

102°W

The Moose Mountain wheel is dominated by the great cairn at its centre, which is about 20 feet (6m) across and contains at least 60 tons of rock. It is ringed by a circle of stones.

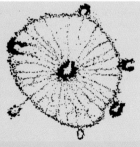

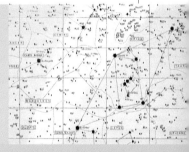

The most convincing celestial alignment at Moose Mountain links the central cairn and the longest of the spokes (above) with sunrise on the summer solstice.

The Big Horn boulder outline (above) has, like Moose Mountain, a number of smaller cairns around its circumference. The astronomer John A. Eddy has discovered that the position of the outer cairns in relation to the central cairn is almost the same as in that of the Moose Mountain wheel.

The theory that the Moose Mountain wheel was a celestial calendar is based on possible star alignments in the past 2,000 years. For example, if the wheel was made between AD1 and AD1000, one spoke would have aligned with the rising of Sirius, the brightest star in the constellation Canis Major (above).

Standing stones

Four hundred people were needed to re-erect this 187-ton menhir at Plabennec, Brittany.

Standing stones, dug out of the landscape, dragged to sites at varying distances from their places of origin and set upright for obscure purposes, have an almost anthropomorphic quality. Almost inevitably, folk legends have crowded around them – as they always do around a monument once its pur-

pose has been forgotten. A typical story is the Cornish tale of young women being transformed into the stone circle called the Merry Maidens in punishment for dancing on the Sabbath.

The term megalith is applied to any prehistoric, massive, undressed block of stone, of the kind widely erected in northwest European landscapes during the period 3200–1500BC. A menhir (from the Breton *men*, "stone", and *hir*, "long") was a type of megalith – a simple upright stone of the type most often found in western Europe, particularly Brittany, either alone or as part of a whole complex, such as a circle, half-circle or alignment.

Many menhirs were large enough to command the landscape. In Brittany, the Grand Menhir Brisé, which today lies in pieces on the ground, was once almost 70 feet (22m) high.

The quarrying of standing stones was an operation requiring great ingenuity in an age of primitive tools. It is possible that wedges of timber were forced into cracks in the rock and soaked with water, causing them to expand and widen the split. Another likely technique was the lighting of fires along fault lines, followed by a sudden cold soaking. Transportation was laborious.

LIVING MEMORIALS

An ancient tradition of erecting megaliths as burial monuments and for other commemorative purposes has continued into modern times in the southern hemisphere.

In the 18th century, the king of Ambohimanga in Madagascar ordered a stone to be erected in celebration of his marriage; it took two months to transport the megalith from its mountain location. In 1907, a Dutch

colonial adminstrator photographed a megalith being erected on the island of Nias near Sumatra in Southeast Asia, intended as a home for a tribal chief's spirit. As recently as 1960 several stones were erected to celebrate Madagascar's independence from France.

In some parts of Madagascar, even quite recent stones are seen as phalluses, and women hoping to have children try to throw pebbles on top of them, believing that if they succeed in their aim, their prayers will be answered.

CONSECRATED STONES

Many ancient stone formations were destroyed by the Church in France and Britain, and as late as 1560 a stone circle on the Scottish island of Iona, reputed to have a sacrificial victim buried under each of 12 stones, was destroyed. Other monuments survived because

A standing stone or menhir converted to a Christian shrine.

they were in church grounds—for example the stone circle in the cemetery of Midmar Kirk, Aberdeenshire.

However, old legends live on. The belief that standing stones are a source of fertility and healing powers has inspired many people to visit the churchyard of La Pierre de Saint Martin in Pitres, France, where they tie pieces of cloth on a Christian cross which stands in front of a solitary megalith.

The most impressive megalithic alignments are at Carnac in Brittany, the site of more than 3,000 prehistoric stone monuments. Quarried from local granite, the stones were commandeered for ritual purposes by the Romans, who carved some of them with images of the Roman gods. Other, similar alignments are found in smaller densities in southwest England (there are 60 or so on Dartmoor), and even as far afield as southeast Asia. Some rows end in circular or rectangular stone configurations; others end with a single stone set at right angles to the main axis. It has been suggested that these end-stones were in some way intended to block the passage of the spirits of the dead. A parallel to this is the use of low walls inside the gateways to temples in Indonesia, to obstruct the spirits, which can move only in straight lines.

The purpose of prehistoric standing stones is obscure, and it is difficult to chart a confident course between conflicting speculations, many of them relating to astronomy, fertility, the Mother Goddess and sacred ritual.

A 19th-century imaginative reconstruction of the stone alignments at Carnac, France.

Although weathering has made its mark over the centuries, even at the time of erection it is probable that each stone had its unique character, and here and there one cannot help seeing in a particular set of surfaces and indentations a human or animal face. This idea has led some experts to suppose that some of the stones may have been intended as images of the gods.

The great circles

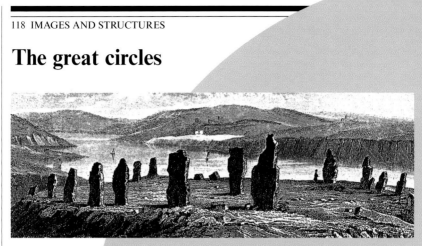

The Ring of Brodgar, Orkney, has a henge and an inner circle which once contained 60 stones.

The stone circles of the Neolithic period in northwest Europe are so deeply bound up with their landscapes that they seem almost to have grown out of the earth. Standing on windswept moors and pastures, they resemble vast open-air temples or ritual enclosures. Although no evidence of their function has been unearthed, it has been speculated that they were originally used for pagan sacrifices, Druidic ceremonies or mother goddess worship.

One megalithic complex, at Callanish on the Isle of Lewis in the Outer Hebrides, off Scotland, acts, in association with its surrounding landscape, as a vast lunar calendar. In its 19-year cycle the moon at its most southerly point appears to skim the horizon when seen from the prehistoric site. The great stone circle of Stonehenge in southern England (see pp.122–3) also has celestial associations: at dawn on the summer solstice

Callanish, on the Isle of Lewis, Scotland, is remarkable for its lunar alignments.

an obsever standing in the centre of Stonehenge will see the sun rise over the heel stone, situated outside the circle. Nobody knows what purpose this astronomical relationship fulfilled. However, one British civil engineer, after measuring hundreds of megalithic sites, has claimed that all the major stone circles in Britain are related in some way to the phases of the moon, and in some cases may have helped ancient peoples to predict the movements of the tides. Beyond doubt is the great importance that these henges must have held for those who built them, since an enormous effort was required by the small and scattered population in order to quarry, transport and erect the huge megaliths. The motivating impulse must have been intense, akin to something like missionary zeal.

Long after the original functions of these sites had been forgotten, they continued to be centres of activity and often controversy. The Romans used Maumbury Rings in Dorset as an amphitheatre; and in the 1640s, during the English Civil War, this site shielded Parliamentary troops. A village sprang up in the centre of Avebury (see pp.120–21), which now grapples with the sometimes conflicting demands of a village economy, tourism and conservation. Stonehenge is a focus of dispute as fears for its safety have led to a ban on Druids and other neo-pagans from celebrating the summer solstice there.

Maumbury Rings, a Neolithic henge near Dorchester in Dorset, southern England.

THE ROLLRIGHT STONES

On a limestone ridge in Oxfordshire stand the remains of a large stone circle known as the Rollright Stones (above).

Erosion has broken many of the limestone slabs, and some have been carried away for other building purposes. However, the circle survives intact, measuring more than 100 feet (nearly 30m) in diameter, and some of the monoliths are more than 6 feet (2m) high.

Stories of this mysterious circle abound. According to William Camden's *Britannia*, published in the 17th century, local people believed that the stones were once a group of knights and their king. In one account, a witch turned the king into the King Stone, a large monolith 75 feet (245m) from the circle, and his men into the circle itself. In Tudor times the rocks were said to be a well-known meeting place for witches.

Avebury, southern England

Avebury is a massive Neolithic henge monument which stands on a low rise above level ground on the Marlborough Downs in Wiltshire, southern England. It encloses part of the modern village of Avebury. The henge (*c*.2600–*c*.2300BC) consists of two general features: the ditch together with its encircling bank, and a number of megalithic circles and other standing stones. The excavation of the ditch would have been an arduous task, as an estimated 200,000 tons of rough chalk gravel had to be scrabbled out with antler picks. The stones, weighing as much as 40 tons, were dragged or sledded a distance of nearly two miles from Avebury Down.

The earthwork has survived largely intact, but the standing stones have suffered from centuries of abuse at the hands of those who lived among them. As early as the 14th century, stones were being toppled and buried, possibly owing to the influence of the medieval Church, which regarded the monument as a temple to paganism. The skeleton of a man, still with three 14th-century coins in his possession, was found under the edge of one stone.

The destruction of Avebury reached its height at the beginning of the 18th century, and by the mid-19th century no more than 20 out of almost 200 stones were still standing. As a result, detailed knowledge of Avebury's megaliths depends on early maps, together with modern archaeological excavations and geophysical surveys.

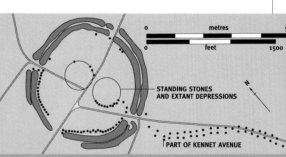

STANDING STONES AND EXTANT DEPRESSIONS

PART OF KENNET AVENUE

Avebury's circular bank is some 1,396 feet (427m) in diameter and rises to a height of almost 20 feet (6m). A narrow berm (ledge) separates it from a ditch as much as 33 feet (10m) deep and more than 65 feet (20m) across. The enclosure is broken by four entrances – the northwest entrance is shown here with raised causeways crossing the ditch.

The massive stone circle at Avebury is more than 539 feet (165m) in diameter and consists of at least 98 huge sarsens, 27 of which stand today. This structure encloses two smaller circles, each about 340 feet (104m) in diameter. The south circle had 34 or more stones; five survive and a soil resistivity survey detected 12 sockets where stones had once stood. A giant monolith

once stood inside the south circle; it was removed in the 18th century. In the north circle, only four of at least 26 stones have survived.

The great circle of the ditch at Avebury is etched deeply into the Wiltshire countryside. Whereas the monument was once defined simply by ditch, bank and stones, together with the great megalithic avenues which extended out across hills and valleys, it is now marked by trees and cut by roads. The village of Avebury, crowded in the centre of the henge, breached the earthwork long ago and has spread into the fields to the west. A slender meandering row of trees shows the course of the Winterbourne stream from the village to the conical mound of Silbury Hill (see pp.106–7), which rises from the patch-work of cultivated fields.

Many people believe that Avebury was built as a monument to an ancient Earth goddess. Today those who hold such views gather at the site in order to meditate in an endeavour to attune themselves to the rhythms of the natural world.

The Kennet Avenue, shown here, is formed by a double row of massive megaliths. It is almost 50 feet (15m) wide and connects Avebury with the Sanctuary, a small stone circle, now destroyed, to the southeast. Each pair of stones has one tall thin pillar and one that is shorter and broader, possibly a design expressing some long-forgotten (perhaps male and female) symbolism.

Beckhampton Avenue was an avenue of standing stones which once led from an entrance of the henge toward a stream. By 1800 the Avenue had been demolished but a small megalithic construction known as the Cove still stands beside it, a mile (1.6km) from Avebury. The two remaining stones of the Cove, shown here, have been dubbed Adam and Eve.

Stonehenge, southern England

The ruins of Stonehenge, a great Neolithic monument on Salisbury Plain in Wiltshire, represent the last of several forms taken by the monument over many centuries. Beginning *c*.3000BC as a simple ditch and bank, by *c*.2100BC it had superseded Avebury to the north as southern England's main ritual centre.

The monument was believed from early times to have calendrical significance. It was observed some time ago that the avenue to the northeast of the henge, with its "heel" stone, aligns with sunrise on the summer solstice, a fact that has been taken as evidence of sun worship; it is possible that there was originally a winter solstice alignment also. An American astronomer, Gerald Hawkins, suggested in the 1960s that Stonehenge was a complex instrument for predicting the times of solar and lunar eclipses.

The construction of Stonehenge, no less than its astronomical sophistication, has been an object of wonder. In the second phase of building, about eighty bluestone pillars were brought to the site (possibly by sea and along the River Avon) from the Preseli Mountains in southwest Wales, a distance of about 240 miles (385km): one folk legend claimed that these non-local stones were brought to Stonehenge by magic. It is possible that the mountain whence they came had sacred significance.

There is little evidence to support the belief that the so-called Altar Stone, a dressed sarsen in the centre of the henge, was originally used for sacrifice. It may simply be a toppled upright.

HOLES
NORTH BARROW
HEEL
SOUTH BARROW
SLAUG STONE
BANK
DITCH

51°11'N
ATLANTIC OCEAN
UK
Poland
Germany
France
Austria
1°51'W
Italy

Stonehenge at the end of the 19th century, before the re-erection of many of the stones, such as the tilted megalith in the centre of the picture.

The Ancient Order of Druids (founded in the 19th century) celebrates the midsummer dawn. William Stukeley first proposed in the 1720s that Stonehenge was a Druid temple: earlier it had been seen as Roman or Danish. The Druids initiated over 600 priests here in 1905 and until recently the summer solstice ceremony was the focus of the Druid year.

A plan of the entire complex of Stonehenge. The oldest part of the monument, the outer bank and ditch henge of c.3000BC, encloses the megalithic structures erected nearly a millennium later. Although a number of graves have been found within the monument, there is no direct evidence for an old tradition that human sacrifice took place at the site.

Circles and humps around Stonehenge constitute an entire spiritualized landscape.

The central part of the monument, after restoration. Many of the stones had fallen or were missing; eleven have been straightened and six re-erected. Only seven of the megaliths at Stonehenge have never been disturbed. The outer sarsen circle would originally have consisted of 30 stones with a continuous lintel, and the inner "horseshoe" of five trilithons (see right).

An imaginative 18th-century impression of how Stonehenge may have looked in its heyday during a great Druidic festival. However, the henge, like many other prehistoric monuments formerly attributed to the ancient Britons, predates the Celtic presence in southern Britain.

A trilithon consists of two stone pillars topped by a horizontal capstone. The five trilithons at the centre of Stonehenge were dressed smooth and secured by mortise-and-tenon joints. The central trilithon (above) is the tallest, measuring 10 feet (3m) wide and more than 25 feet (8m) high.

Lost megalithic cultures

The remains of a prehistoric taula *(the term means "table" in the local language, Catalan) on Minorca. The function of these unusual structures is unknown, but they may have been religious.*

Bronze Age cultures that flourished in the western Mediterranean in the 2nd millennium BC have left mysterious megalithic remains in the Balearic Islands and on Sardinia. These ancient cultures were probably unrelated, but in both cases their builders were skilled craftsmen who erected imposing structures of finely dressed granite, limestone or basalt blocks that fitted together without mortar.

On Majorca and Minorca there were once thousands of the limestone towers known as *talayots*, the vestiges of a culture that evidently continued into Roman times. A great many of them were destroyed by the spread of agriculture, but where they survive they usually stand in groups, sometimes enclosed by a wall. They look like fortified compounds, but their original use is a mystery. Whereas some have small chambers within the thickness of their walls, many others are solid. It has been suggested that they may have been defences against invasion, or funerary monuments, or simply the foundations of buildings that have decayed with age. On Minorca a *talayot* usually stands within a stone enclosure and is accompanied by a *taula*, a massive upright slab of dressed stone upon which

SU NURAXI

A large, isolated hill covered with scattered stones once rose above a plain at Su Nuraxi near the village of Barumini in south-central Sardinia. However, after a violent thunderstorm, floodwater washed away the soil and revealed that the hill was actually an enormous *nuraghe*, flanked by four large towers and several smaller ones connected by a wall. The structure stood amid dozens of small, mainly circular buildings resembling toadstools.

Archaeological excavation suggests that Su Nuraxi was built in phases over several centuries, with the main tower constructed *c.*1500BC, the four flanking towers *c.*1200BC, the enclosing wall *c.*900BC and the remaining structures after that. Research indicates that the settlement was destroyed by the Carthaginians in the 6th century BC.

another has been laid horizontally to form a T-shaped structure. It is widely believed that the *taulas* had some ritual function or were central supports for ceremonial halls. Most of the information about the people who built these structures comes from the *navetas* or *naus* (Catalan for "ships"), stone tombs resembling an upside-down boat which were constructed near the *talayots*. The *navetas* have yielded the remains of many dead together with their burial goods, including early Bronze Age pottery and copper and bronze objects.

The *nuraghe*, a prehistoric conical tower built from great blocks of volcanic basalt or granite, is a common sight on Sardinia. It is generally accepted that the island's 7,000 or so *nuraghi*, concentrated in the south-central and northwestern regions, were built between *c.*1500BC and *c.*400BC. They were clearly occupied, because they contain chambers with vaulted or flat ceilings and spiral staircases leading to upper stories. Possibly for defensive reasons, each *nuraghe* is visible from at least one other. The largest *nuraghi* are more than 45 feet (14m) in diameter and 65 feet (20 m) high, with walls up to 15 feet (4.5m) thick. Among artefacts found in them are tools, weapons and domestic utensils. Other objects, of clay, metal and obsidian, may have had a religious purpose. At Serra Orrios, a *nuraghe* village near Dorgali, there are nearly eighty buildings, including temples and a theatre.

The Naveta d'es Tudons on Minorca, one of the oldest roofed buildings in Europe.

Machu Picchu, Peru

During the expansion of the Inca empire in the 15th century AD, a number of small citadels were built high above the gorge of the Urubamba River 60 miles (100km) to the northwest of Cuzco, the Inca capital, in Peru. One of these towns was Machu Picchu, a settlement of stone-built palaces, temples, plazas and houses perched on a saddle-shaped ridge between the pinnacles of Huayna Picchu ("New Picchu") and Machu Picchu ("Old Picchu"). It is surrounded on most sides by a steep drop.

The town consists of an outer and an inner sector: the latter, entered by a single gateway, appears to be the religious quarter, since it contains buildings which seem once to have had a sacred function. One such building stands on top of a granite outcrop which has been sculpted inside the building into a shrine or altar. Beneath the outcrop is a grotto fashioned out of a natural overhang, within which a number of Inca mummies have been found.

Some authorities believe that Machu Picchu was simply a medium-sized fortified town remarkable chiefly for its extraordinary state of preservation. But the town's isolation and the sacred sites within its walls have inspired other theories about its original purpose. One suggestion is that it was a religious sanctuary for the Acclas ("Chosen Women"), an élite of female devotees of the sun god Inti. Around 170 rich burials have been found at Machu Picchu, of which 150 were of women.

Machu Picchu is built mainly of white granite. Its architects overcame the problem of building with a difficult material in an awkward location by laying the stones so that they diminished in size as they rose, producing walls that taper and lean inwards. The city was abandoned when it was less than a century old as the Inca empire fell to the Conquistadors.

Seen through every door and window in the town, the spectacular valley of the Urubamba River drops steeply away. The Inca stonemasons used stone hammers to dress the granite blocks into irregular shapes with such precision that they fitted together without mortar.

The Spanish Conquistadors never reached Machu Picchu on account of its isolated position. It was thus remarkably intact when the American archaeologist Hiram Bingham rediscovered it in 1911.

In spite of the severe slope, cultivation terraces, as seen above and far left, rise more than 1,000 feet (300m) up into the centre of the town. Their retaining walls rise nearly 12 feet (3.5m) for every 10 feet (3m) of land for crops.

The massive shrine called the Torreón was skilfully sculpted out of a solid granite overhang. The coursed masonry and sculpted steps have been perfectly integrated into the surrounding space, despite the cramped and angular surfaces.

The inti-huatana, *or "hitching place of the sun", rises more than 6 feet (2m) above the natural outcrop in the main temple complex. Such monoliths are a feature of several Inca temples: they are connected with sun worship or solar observation. This is the only one to survive intact: the others were destroyed by the Spanish as pagan monuments.*

Pyramids

The middle of the third millennium BC was an Egyptian golden age, reflected in the many royal funerary pyramids built on the west bank of the Nile. These were the places from which the pharaohs (kings) whose mummified corpses were placed inside them began their journey into the afterlife. Texts inscribed inside the pyramids suggest the reason for their striking form and scale: the spirits of the deceased kings would use the rays of the sun, whose geometry the pyramids echo, as a ramp whereby to reach the sky.

In the 13th century BC the impact of these monuments was compromised when the white polished limestone which originally covered their steep sides began to be quarried for building material. Yet today the pyramids are still hugely impressive, both for their engineering achievement and for their connotations of spiritual energy.

The architectural form that eventually gave rise to the Egyptian pyramids had its inception as the simple mastaba,

The pyramids and the Great Sphinx at Giza.

an enclosed open-air courtyard beneath which lay the chambers of the dead. Almost 5,000 years ago, during the reign of Zoser in the Third Dynasty, a celebrated architect, Imhotep, designed a radically new tomb for the king at Saqqara: by piling a sequence of six successively smaller mastabas one on top of the other he created a step pyramid. For the next 500 years, step pyramids grew in size and their sides became smoother until, in the reign of Khufu, the greatest of all these monuments rose out of the sands at Giza.

In Mesopotamia, from the late 3rd to the 1st millennium BC, millions of bricks were baked and cemented with bitumen in order to form pyramidic models of the cosmos called ziggurats. The ziggurat was a step pyramid with corners set at the cardinal directions and a main staircase running from the base to a shrine at the top. It may have been seen as a symbol of the primeval mound that was believed to have existed before the earth and sky were separated at the beginning of creation; if so,

The "Pyramid of the Niches" at El Tajin, Mexico, had 365 niches which were somehow related to the days of the solar year.

PYRAMID POWER

In the Middle Ages, star-worshipping cults conducted rituals in cavernous chambers deep in the heart of the Great Pyramid of Giza, seeing the vast monument as a source of wisdom. In the 1970s and 1980s, many Westerners became intrigued by esoteric theories and attempted to harness the allegedly mystical power of the pyramid by building their own pyramids, whether from cardboard, plastic, or some other easily obtainable modern material. Believing that the shape of the space inside the pyramid contained the secret of its power, they would sit under pyramids while meditating, praying or undergoing therapy. A Czech radio engineer, Karel Drbal, claimed that storing razor blades under a cardboard pyramid kept them sharp for as many as 200 shaves, and took out a Czech patent for his "Cheops Pyramid Razor Blade Sharpener". Others were convinced that vegetables would stay fresh longer, or dehydrate without spoiling, if stored inside a pyramid-shaped box.

The pyramid at this sacred ceremony in Brazil is believed to act as a focus and magnifier of spiritual energy.

it may have been regarded as an abode of the gods.

After the Near Eastern sites, the best-known pyramids are those of Meso-america, usually built of earth and faced with stone. Typically, they are stepped, with a platform or temple structure on the summit. At Chichén Itzá, a Maya city in Mexico which flourished from the late 10th to 13th centuries, the Castillo pyramid rises almost 82 feet (25m) in height. Its nine terraces, symbolizing the nine underground worlds of the Mayan cosmos, lead up to a simple rectangular temple. Priests would ascend the pyramid's steep staircase to perform sacrifices to their gods. Bas-reliefs found here depict bearded men believed to show priests of the snake-god Quetzalcoatl.

Solar orientations have been identified in many Egyptian and Mesoamerican pyramids, reflecting an interest in astronomy and the calendar. The similarities between pyramids from such

A 16th-century illustration of Aztec prisoners of war sacrificed to the sun on a temple pyramid.

different cultural contexts also reflect certain engineering requirements: the pyramid form combined great height with structural stability. Massive in scale, these monuments provided evidence of the great power of the élites which built them.

The Great Pyramid, Giza, Egypt

The Great Pyramid of Khufu (or Cheops) rises from the desert sands of a royal cemetery built during the Fourth Dynasty (*c.*2613–*c.*2494BC) at Giza, near present-day Cairo. It is constructed out of massive blocks of limestone, each weighing more than two tons, which were chiselled into shape by gangs of stonemasons and dragged from a local quarry along great causeways and ramps to the pyramid site. According to the Greek historian Herodotus (*c.*485–425BC), the pyramid took thirty years to complete. Generations of workers laid more than two million blocks on a base 756 feet (230m) square to reach the pyramid's original height of 481 feet (147m).

Little is known of the life of the pharoah Khufu, but his name appears on monuments across Egypt, and members of his entourage built their own temples and tombs around his pyramid. The second largest of the three pyramids at Giza contained the remains of his son, Khafre (or Khephren).

Like all Egyptian kings, Khufu was revered as divine, and people wore amulets inscribed with his sacred name. His reign was still recalled in the Ptolemaic period, over 2,000 years after his death, but his pyramid received less respect. It was broken into and looted, probably during the unrest that occurred when the Old Kingdom collapsed (*c.*2181BC). In the following centuries, the pyramids at Giza were quarried as a source of stone for new monuments.

*The Great Sphinx, a statue of a human-headed lion, is thought to have been built in order to guard the pyramid of Khafre (*c.*2520BC).*

The image of Khufu's burial monument and its perfect geometric shape have become worldwide symbols of the heroic defiance of death, the presumption of the living, the endurance of civilizations, the irretrievable nature of past faiths, and the psychic power of abstract geometry.

The interior of the pyramid has several cramped passageways leading to the burial chambers and a tunnel cut by the Muslim Caliph Mamun in the 9th century.

The pyramids at Giza are the only one of the Seven Wonders of the Ancient World still extant. Plundering for limestone left the Great Pyramid 30 feet (9m) shorter than when it was built.

The entrance to the pyramid gives way to a sloping passage at the bottom of which is an unfinished chamber: the intended burial place. Before completing this chamber, the builders apparently changed their plans and built an ascending passage. They then built a third passage, rising almost to the centre of the pyramid. This was Khufu's final burial place.

The passage leading to the entrance to the pharoah Khufu's burial chamber is a massive gallery, 154 feet (47m) long and nearly 30 feet (9m) high, with a corbelled roof. In the burial chamber lay the pharaoh's mummified corpse.

In their initiation ceremonies, Freemasons call on the sacred power of the pyramids, depicted on the Masonic emblem, above. According to ancient occult lore, a pyramid represents life and spiritual resurrection. It unites the triangle (a symbol of cosmic trinities such as birth, life and death) and the square (a symbol of the four quarters of the universe).

Worlds in living rock

Valleys once filled with volcanic ash in the region of central Anatolia known as Cappadocia have been eroded into an eerie wasteland of strange conical formations, sometimes standing alone, sometimes huddled together like hooded monks. The first outsider to describe this remote and unearthly region did so in the late 18th century when, sent by the French court to explore the lands of the Mediterranean, he wrote of seeing "pyramidical houses". Later explorers confirmed that houses were indeed hollowed out of the cones and were lived in by troglodytes (cave-dwellers), who continued to scratch out a living in the well-watered but infertile valleys. Even more remarkable than the rock-cut dwellings, stables and pigeon houses is the region's great quantity of rock-cut churches, small chapels and stark, cramped cells where a thousand years ago monks and other Christian hermits devoted their lives to solitary prayer.

Rock-cut caves express the desire for unity between the human spirit and the ancient body of the Earth. At Ajanta in India, between the 2nd century BC and the 5th century AD, generations of devout Buddhists created sacred space in solid rock by carving out cave temples and filling them with scenes of the life of the Buddha (see pp.134–5).

In the late 6th century, Hindus created a great cave temple to the god Shiva on Elephant Island in Bombay har-

Caves carved in the weird formations caused by the weathering of volcanic rock in Cappadocia.

THE HERMITAGE OF NIKETAS THE STYLITE

The arched entrance to a hollowed cone on the slopes of Güllü Dere (the Rose-Pink Valley) in Cappadocia leads to a small chapel lit by a single square window. The walls of the chapel are covered with images of saints and apostles, the Virgin and Child and the Crucifixion. Also in the chapel is a dedication to a monk called Niketas. Like St Symeon, whose image apears nearby, Niketa was a stylite: a Christian ascetic who lived on the top of a pillar (in Greek, *stylos*).

Above the chapel, near the top of the cone, rock has fallen away to reveal a small chamber. This cramped room, which has a cross carved on its ceiling, is thought to be where Niketas lived on his pillar a thousand years ago. The chamber would have been accessible only by ladder or by precarious footholds carved into the outside wall leading up to an opening at the top of the cone.

An artist's impression of a stylite.

bour. The main temple has a pillared nave which leads to a linga, a phallus-shaped symbol of the god (see pp.22–3). Adjoining this central area of worship are smaller cave shrines with sculptures illustrating scenes from the life of the god. In remoter areas of northern China, the Buddhist fervour which swept the countryside from the 4th century AD inspired similar complexes. Near Mai-chishan, or Corn Rick Mountain, a cave temple developed at the site of a naturally formed stupa, an earthen mound or hill regarded as a mortuary

Houses carved out of the red sandstone at Petra, Jordan.

shrine to the Buddha. Over hundreds of years the cliff face has become honey-combed with individual chambers, from simple niches to pillared shrines with vaulted ceilings. Earthquakes and the weathering of friable rock have caused some shrines to collapse, but many still contain clay statues of the Buddha and his attendants as well as those of other Buddhist divinities and worshippers.

One of the most spectacular cave churches is ad-Dayr ("The Monastery"), converted in Byzantine times from an unfinished tomb façade in the sandstone city of Petra, Jordan.

The spectacular rock-cut tombs of the ancient city of Petra, Jordan. Most of the extant architecture dates from c.100BC to c.AD150. Classical façades reflect close trading links with the Hellenistic world.

Ajanta, central India

The twenty-nine cave temples of Ajanta in central India were carved into the sheer face of a meandering, horseshoe-shaped gorge on the Waghora River. They are the work of Buddhists, who used them as retreats from the 2nd century BC to the 5th century AD. Many of the Ajanta caves have carved, pillared entrances and interior sculptures, but their most striking features are the frescoes which cover almost all the walls and ceilings.

The paintings were all made with the same pigments and have complementary themes. Different subjects were painted in different parts of the chamber: images of the Buddha near the antechambers and shrines; and *jatakas* (popular tales of the Buddha's previous incarnations) in the principal halls.

Ceilings were painted in geometric patterns with intertwined animal and plant motifs suggesting the gardens of paradise. This unified conception suggests a profoundly holistic view of the cosmos. One scene, painted in the 1st century BC, shows a prince and his entourage walking toward a sacred tree where musicians accompany two lively dancers; another, in a late 5th century *vihara*, a cave in which monks both lived and worshipped, shows a prince called Mahajanaka surrounded by beautiful women. The initial impression of both of these narratives is strongly secular, although the first depicts a sacred ritual and the second shows the prince at the moment of renouncing his worldly life for that of a religious recluse.

A cross-section of one of the temples (above), showing the elaborate architectural designs that were cut into the solid rock of the cliff face. The temples were discovered in 1824, some 1,500 years after they had been abandoned. By then, these brightly painted retreats had deteriorated into dark and damp caves – overgrown, vandalized and inhabited only by animals. One of the sculpted panels on the left of the cross-section is shown in more detail on the opposite page (far right). *The painters at Ajanta used natural earth ochres and the blue of lapis lazuli in their work. Some of the paintings are relatively restrained scenes of the Buddha preaching, but those depicting events from his previous lives and from the jataka folktales are often sensual and worldly – crowded, as above, with richly dressed and graceful people.*

Lieutenant James Alexander, a British officer of the 16th Lancers, gave an account of his discovery of Ajanta in February 1824: "With our pistols cocked we ascended by the branch of a tree to the upper range of chambers; and found, in the middle of one of the floors, the remains of a recent fire, with large foot-marks around it. In the corner was the entire skeleton of a man. On the floor of many of the lower caves I observed the prints of the feet of tigers, jackals, bears, monkeys, pea-cocks etc.; these were impressed upon the dust, formed by the plaster of the fresco paintings which had fallen from the ceilings."
The entrance to cave nine (left) leads into one of the many halls lining the gorge.

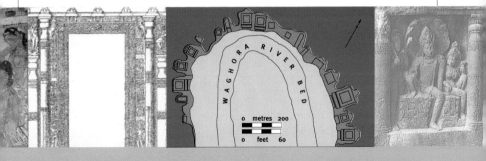

The jambs and lintel of the door to cave six (above) are intricately carved with figures, leaves and animals. The door opens into the lower shrine.

The caves extend around the semicircular cliff face of a scarp on the Waghora River. The scarp is about 250 feet (80m) high. Caves were excavated roughly side by side, varying in elevation from about 35 feet (10m) to 100 feet (30m) above the river. They are numbered consecutively from right to left for archaeological purposes.

The statue above depicts nagas, semi-divine serpent beings who are said to live in wonderful jewelled palaces in an underwater city, Bhagavati. The chief naga, shown here, is called Naganaja.

Underground temples and tombs

The Romans performed rituals in honour of Mithra, the ancient Persian god of light, in dark caves and subterranean chambers. This underground setting was determined by their belief that Mithra had slain a great ox in a cave after emerging from a rock with a sword and a flaming torch, and then

Rectangular burial slots in the rock tomb of Mada'in Salih, Saudi Arabia.

making peace with the sun. The slaughter of the bull symbolized how life emerged from death in the womb-like darkness of the earth, for the blood and body of the beast were believed to be the source of all animals and plants. Every Mithraeum, or temple of Mithra, was a gloomy refuge which brought together images of life and death, darkness and light, earth and sky: the bull was carved on the altar, and on the ceiling were painted images of the sun, moon and planets. Worshippers would gather in the Mithraeum and consume the blood and flesh of a sacrificial bull in the hope of gaining immortality.

The cult of Mithra celebrated the idea that the end of human life was the beginning of another journey, in step with the rhythms of the natural world. This belief has been expressed in the burial traditions of a wide range of differing cultures.

The hope of an afterlife is clearly expressed in the design and location of some burial chambers. Oval burial mounds built 2,000 years ago in what is now the Central African Republic, and topped by standing stones, are sited near springs so that the dead would never be far from water. At Newgrange, a great tomb constructed near the River Boyne in Ireland during the 3rd millennium BC (see pp.138–9), the rising sun on the winter solstice finds its way through an opening above the entrance for a brief moment – perhaps intended to provide light for the dead on the darkest day of the year.

An early expression of the Christian cult of the dead was the catacomb (subterranean cemetery) in which funeral feasts (with a Eucharist) were held on the burial day and on anniversaries.

The interior of the Aztec temple of Malinalco, hewn from the rock and used by worshippers in the 15th and 16th centuries AD.

SHIP BURIALS

According to many cultures, the dead had to travel at least part of the journey to their home in the afterlife by boat, sometimes encountering a figure such as Charon, the grim-faced boatman who, according to ancient Greek mythology, would ferry them across the River Styx into the underworld. In some cultures, the boats needed by the dead were provided as part of the burial goods. Egyptian kings and noblemen sometimes had cedar boats buried alongside their tombs in the hope that this would enable them to accompany the sun god on his daily journey across the sky. Anglo-Saxon and Viking kings and chieftains some-times chose to be buried inside the boats that they believed would carry them to eternity.

In the late 1930s archaeologists excavated a low mound at Sutton Hoo on the coast of Suffolk in England, and discovered a ship grave of the Anglo-Saxon period. The ship (only the impression of which remained) had been over 25 feet (82m) long, with a hull of overlapping planks. Although no trace of a body was found, the burial yielded a fabulous treasure of gold, silver, bronze, iron and precious stones, all of which had been used to decorate weaponry, armour, clothing, a lyre, drinking flasks and other utensils, coins and jewelry. This was clearly the grave of a high status, probably royal, individual. It is widely believed to be that of Rædwald, a king of the East Angles who died c.AD624.

A reconstruction of the helmet found at Sutton Hoo.

SETTINGS FOR THE DEAD

Although some burial places symbolize the body's subjection to natural cycles by their location in wilderness settings, others create a more formal, artificial world as a final resting place for the deceased.

The Mughal emperors of India chose elaborate and highly structured gardens as the settings for opulent pavilions. When the emperors died, the pavilions became tombs and the gardens were opened to the public, who could then pay homage to the dead man.

The gardens of the Taj Mahal, built AD1631-53 for the wife of a Mughal emperor, are intended to represent the gardens of paradise on the day of resurrection. At the gateway to the gardens a sign reads: "These are the gardens of Eden, enter them to live forever!"

In the 20th century, in the face of increasing urbanization, cemeteries often became a means whereby nature could be brought into cities. For example, Woodland Cemetery outside Stockholm was designed by Gunnar Asplund (1885-1940) in reaction to the rapid increase in population of the Swedish capital. In a bid to capture the spirit of a romanticized past, Asplund incorporated native pine forests into his setting, and for the funerary structures within the cemetery he looked for inspiration to the Classical world. The wooded summit of a hill was set aside for meditation, recalling the groves of ancient Greece.

A chambered tomb at Pentre Ifan, South Wales, isolated in its wild landscape.

Newgrange, Ireland

Newgrange is a massive chambered tomb or passage-grave built more than 5,000 years ago on a bend of the River Boyne in County Meath, Ireland. It shares its landscape with two other large passage graves at Dowth to the east and Knowth to the west, as well as a number of smaller earthen enclosures.

Inside the tomb, a narrow passage leads to the main chamber, which opens up into a corbelled, or beehive-shaped, vault with three flat-roofed chambers forming a cross pattern. Bone fragments of at least four people, two of whom were cremated, have been found in the tomb floor nearby.

At some point the sides of the tomb collapsed, concealing the entrance. The remains of late Neolithic-early Bronze Age living sites with hearths were found around the entrance area.

In 1972 Professor M. O'Kelly discovered a "roof box" above the entrance – that is, a structure positioned so as to allow a beam of sunlight to fall, at sunrise on midwinter day, on the triple spiral design in the burial chamber, more than 600 feet (180m) inside.

Newgrange evidently remained of significance in Celtic times, because gold and other ornaments inspired by or imported from Roman Britain, together with Roman coins, were found in the tomb. They were probably offerings to the spirits of the place. The prehistoric burial mounds entered Irish myth and folklore as *sidhe* or fairymounds, the dwellings of fairies and divinities. Newgrange was said to be the home of Oenghus, the god of love.

The mound of turf and stones comprising the tomb at Newgrange rises almost 34 feet (11m) above its surroundings and is nearly 100 yards (90m) across. Skirting the base of the mound are 97 rough-hewn stones laid end to end, the largest of which is almost 16 feet (5m) long. They originally supported a wall of stones about 10 feet (3m) high.

Newgrange is one of the few megalithic monuments with a clear astronomical connection. The central chamber is lit up at dawn on the winter solstice by a thin shaft of sunlight that penetrates through a gap in the entrance.

The 5,000-year-old tomb of Newgrange rises like a stone fortress amid the surrounding Irish pasturelands. Low humps and depressions surrounding the site suggest that other prehistoric monuments may lie buried in what could prove to be a landscape of great sacred significance.

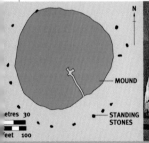

As the above plan shows, Newgrange is surrounded by a circle of standing stones. Twelve of the 35 stones that once made up the circle survive, the largest about 8 feet (2.4m) high. It is not known whether this circle was built at the same time as the mound: it may be associated with an earlier turf mound constructed on the site.

Past the massive entrance stone in the mound at Newgrange is a passage 26 feet (19m) long and 3 feet (1m) wide (above), built of upright stones and roofed by 17 massive capstones. Two of these, at the entrance, weigh more than six tons. The passage gradually increases in height from 5 feet to 6 feet (1.5–2m) nearer the chamber.

Many stones in and around the tomb bear geometric patterns. The entrance to the tomb (above) is behind a large kerbstone covered in spirals, lozenges and concentric arcs, which were pecked into the surface of the stones with flint tools. The spiral has been interpreted as the soul progressing through death to ultimate peace and rebirth.

Ninstints, Queen Charlotte Islands

The abandoned village of Ninstints lies in a sheltered bay on Anthony Island, in the Queen Charlotte Islands group off the Pacific coast of Canada. The sea-going Haida people have occupied these islands for at least 7,000 years, living off the creatures of the ocean, from killer whales to sea urchins, and hunting and gathering in the coastal forests.

Ninstints was the main village of the Kunghit Haida, who occupied the southernmost part of the territory. The Haida called it Sqa'ngwa-i lnaga'i (Red Cod Island Town) after the abundant supply of red snapper caught locally. Its present name is a European corruption of the name of Chief Nanstins (He Who Is Two), who was the last to rule the village before it was abandoned in the late 19th century.

The Kunghit Haida were divided into two large groups, the Eagles and the Ravens. Each group had several clans, each with its own traditions, myths and symbols, many of which were represented on the distinctive totem poles found in Ninstints. The first clan encountered by Europeans was called Those Born At Songs Of Victory Town (see opposite page, below).

When Europeans first came to Ninstints in the 19th century, it was one of thirty to forty villages on the islands. However, within ten years smallpox had decimated the population, while missionary activity and government interference caused severe cultural disruption. By the year 1880 Ninstints had been abandoned, together with all but two Haida towns.

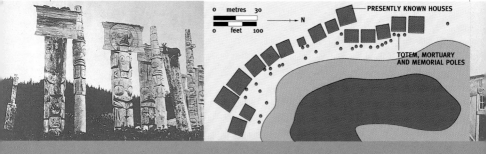

The Haida erected mortuary poles upon which the remains of the dead were contained in cedar boxes.

An archaeological reconstruction of the plan of the village of Ninstints showing the location of houses and their associated totem poles. As well as mortuary poles, the inhabitants of Ninstints erected memorial poles bearing the emblematic crests of people who had died while absent from the village. Each house had a name: the house furthest south was called People Think Of This House Even When They Sleep Because The Master Feeds Everyone Who Calls. Ninstints is a World Heritage Site, recognized as a monument of "exceptional universal value".

Weathered cedar totem poles still stand in front of the remains of houses at Ninstints. The carved figures on the poles represent mythical beings and totemic animals such as bears, ravens and eagles.

Ninstints had a population of more than 300 people who lived in perhaps twenty houses. The houses were large, rectangular frame structures, built entirely of cedar, with vertical posts and large horizontal beams clad in wide planks. The soft, aromatic wood of the red cedar tree provided the Haida with an ideal carving and construction material, resistant to weathering but easily cut and shaped with adzes and other tools.

A carved face decorating a burial chest on top of a mortuary pole. The carvings generally depicted animals associated with the clan of the deceased. This carving is of the moon and the thunderbird, the heraldic crest of the clan Those Born At Songs Of Victory Town.

Working with the Earth

Among those who focus scholarly attention upon the past, students of the spiritualized landscape have a uniquely active relationship with their object of inquiry: they can travel within and among their chosen subject with a rare freedom of movement. The exhilaration of this is partly a matter of scale. Standing in a stone circle, or among rock-cut tombs, we open ourselves up to the larger influences, allowing the enigmas to envelop us.

This concluding section looks at some of the traditions through which we have related actively to the sacred Earth. The shaman makes energetic use of an intensely holistic view of the cosmos to heal the sick, find lost game animals, and deal with other pressing situations. The geomancer works with invisible energy lines in the landscape to create an auspicious framework for daily life. The leyhunter attempts to decode mysterious alignments in the landscape's sacred architecture. The maker of gardens creates a vision of paradise. The astrologer, looking beyond the Earth, seeks a profound understanding of the cosmos.

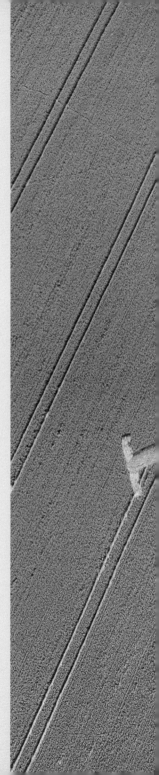

In the late 1980s and early 1990s dozens of circles and other patterns appeared, usually overnight, in cornfields in southern Britain. While it is now known that many of the impressions were created by hoaxers, some people still claim that others were formed by a mysterious earth energy. This circle, photographed on the Marlborough Downs, Wiltshire, on August 5, 1994, resembles a medieval astrological seal.

The shaman's Earth

A South American shaman, Celso Fiallo, blows purifying flames over his altar to keep evil powers at bay.

Among the Matsigenka people of the east-central Peruvian highlands, the shaman travels through a landscape alive with spirits. He may recognize in a certain rock near a river the form of the goddess Pa'reni, mother of fish and game animals, or sense the good spirits who dwell in uplands, lakes and rivers.

This special relationship with the landscape is part of a shaman's ability to deal directly with the spirit world. The shaman may journey in a trance state into the earth or sky to meet and work with spirit helpers or deities. Once in this other world (or altered state of consciousness), shamans may communicate with animal spirits or engage in psychic battles with malevolent influences. On their return to the everyday world, they may have the ability to predict the future, or to help people with problems that occur in the normal course of life, such as illness and emotional difficulties.

Initiates usually enter the shamanic calling after undergoing a sudden and mysterious illness, or an attack of mental instability, or sometimes after experiencing strange and powerful dreams. Thereafter, they find they are capable of entering a state of ecstatic trance, and will develop their gift through a variety of practices. Algonkian shamans prepare themselves to enter the spirit world by going without sleep, water or food,

HEALERS OF PERU

The *curanderos* (Spanish for "healers") of northern coastal Peru draw spiritual power both from the images and rituals of Catholicism and from the experience of hallucinogen mescalin. Through séance and ritual, they attempt to control *encantos*, or the forces of nature. The *curandero* works at a mesa ("table"), an altar covered with a great array of objects arranged in zones which symbolize the different realms of the cosmos.

The left side of the mesa often contains objects associated with the underworld, such as pottery shards from ancient burial grounds, or shells from the sea bed. The right side may contain objects linked to the sky, such as images of saints, herbs from the mountains, or crystals. Stones called *cerros* ("mountains") may also be included in the array, as mountains are believed to be an important source of *encantos*. Opposing cosmic forces are believed to come together at the centre of the mesa, where the healing is carried out.

whereas the Matsigenka shaman finds the paths to the heavens and the underworld after he has drunk a brew made of ayahuasca, a hallucinogenic plant. In southern California a certain Paviotso shaman recounted how he gained his power in a cave: he was attempting to sleep when he heard the sounds of bears, mountain lions and other animals from within the mountain. A crack suddenly appeared in the rock where he lay, and a man emerged who instructed him in the songs necessary to cure sickness, together with various medicines, such as feathers, deer hooves, eagle down and tobacco.

Shamans of Central and South America may attain their trance state by consuming brews derived from hallucinogenic plants such as ayahuasca (left) or the cactus peyote (right).

In Nigeria, Igbo medicine men (a medicine man is essentially a shaman primarily concerned with healing) harness the power of the Earth goddess Ani by using parts of her body, such as clay or the bark and leaves of trees, for divination. In other parts of Africa, novice shamans may undergo months of training in secluded cult houses, from which they emerge transformed, bearing new names to reflect their new role and status in their society.

A Dogon shaman of Mali interprets the meaning of tracks left by a fox over a diagram in the sand.

Geomancy and feng shui

Geomancy has been described as "the science of putting human habitats and activities into harmony with the visible and invisible world". It is believed to have existed in one form or another in most cultures since Neolithic times, and is still part of the traditions of many peoples of Asia, Africa and elsewhere. Geomancy has recently undergone a revival in the urban West among those who look to ancient belief systems in the quest to develop a way of life that pays greater respect to the immanent forces of nature.

According to the highly sophisticated Chinese geomantic system called *feng shui*, two powerful opposing forces run through the Earth: the positive, life-enhancing *chi* and the negative, dangerous *sha*. Each force favours a different physical landscape. In general, evil spirits are believed to move along straight pathways. Mountains and hills are considered to block such lines and to serve as refuges from evil, and as such they attract the desirable force *chi*. The loca-

A Dogon geomancer of Mali interprets the tracks of a mouse on a grid representing the cosmos.

To determine energy lines and other cosmological factors present at a location, a feng shui *master may use a sophisticated magnetic compass (left). It has several concentric rings from which he takes readings.*

tion of a new house, palace, tomb or even an entire city may be decided by a *feng shui* master, who can determine whether the site possesses an auspicious balance of forces. The master's judgment on a proposed site may be critical, for the energy of the site is thought to influence what will happen there in the future. When a new global headquarters for the Hongkong and Shanghai Bank was erected in Hongkong in the 1980s, the owners were careful to consult a *feng shui* master to approve the design and site of their hi-tech skyscraper.

Most Chinese geomancers use the ancient information contained in *feng shui* manuals to calculate earth energies.

FENG SHUI IN BEIJING

Beijing has been modified over the centuries in accordance with *feng shui*.

Mountains protect the city, but many internal features have required alteration. Gates to the north are considered vulnerable because the winds from that direction are said to be dangerous: thus, the northern gate of the walled imperial palace complex (the Forbidden City) is sheltered by an artificial mound known as Prospect Hill.

The required balance between the opposing forces of fire and water was achieved in the southern part of the Forbidden City by means of an artificial stream. It was said to neutralize the "fire" of the southern gate before it reached the "water" of the inner court, at which point the forces become balanced.

The Forbidden City, Beijing (above), was constructed on geomantic principles.

For example, the shape and arrangement of mountains, hills, valleys, plains and other natural features may suggest the outline of an animal, bird or part of the body: this in turn provides a clue to the nature of the invisible forces at work in an area. Rugged, steep land is usually seen as male, and gently undulating land as female. A place surrounded by rolling hills may be interpreted as a crouching tiger – a secure place if the building is located near the tiger's head or paws. Mountain ridges may represent a dragon's back and thus radiate powerful positive energies. Places where these energies are concentrated are known as dragon lairs.

The ideal location, from a *feng shui* master's point of view, is one protected on three sides from negative forces. Beijing is located on a plain, protected

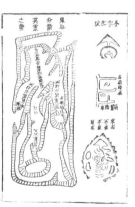

An "energy map" of an area, compiled by a feng shui *master.*

by mountains on the north, east and west; in Fujian, the people of Xiamen attribute their good fortune to the protection offered by two large knolls, Dragon-head Hill and Tiger-head Hill, on either side of the city's inner harbour. A site can be improved by modifying the landscape or placing pagodas at dangerous or unprotected points. Entire buildings might be destroyed or moved to improve the energies; one geomancer from the time of the late Qing dynasty (1644–1911) was so famous for destroying places that he became known as Sun Rake the House Down.

Any disturbance in the landscape is thought to affect its natural energies. For example, when oil drilling began on Hainan Island, South China, residents protested, fearing that it would affect the spiritual harmonies of the area.

Sacred alignments

The main ritual centre of Cuzco, the luca capital, was the Temple of the Sun, from which radiated forty-one sacred lines which can still be traced by plotting the alignment of *huacas* (sites of religious significance). In all there were 328 alignments in the region around Cuzco, matching the number of days in the Inca calendar. Research has shown that some of the lines possessed an astronomical significance, while others were used as ritual paths along which sacrificial victims were carried to their deaths. Some investigators believe that these lines were also used for ritual walking. Every winter, pilgrims are believed to have followed a line running southeast, the direction of the midsummer sun and of the Island of the Sun in Lake

The church of St Michael de Rupe at Brentnor in Devon, west of Dartmoor.

Titicaca 200 miles (320 km) away.

In 1925 Alfred Watkins (1855–1935), a businessman and photographic pioneer, published *The Old Straight Track*, in which he observed that many ancient sites – megalithic monuments, churches, holy wells and cairns – appear to lie on straight alignments for dozens of miles through the English countryside. One alignment in Wiltshire with Salisbury Cathedral near

St Michael's Mount, in Cornwall.

its centre appears to link several prehistoric features including Stonehenge. Watkins discovered that a word which often appears in the names of places lying along these alignments is "ley" (pronounced "lea"), meaning a cleared glade, and so he called these lines "leys". His theory was that they were primarily practical, originating in ancient times as a network of landmarks to guide travellers. The leys passed through prominent hills and mountains where beacons were once lit to mark their course. Watkins' British followers, who formed The Old Straight Track Club, went further, interpreting leys as part of a web of physical and spiritual energy lines, rather like those recognized by Chinese geomancers, running through the terrestrial landscape and ultimately aligning with the stars. One such line, which passes through the Boscawen-un stone circle in Cornwall, near Penzance,

The church of St Michael at Burrow Mump, Somerset.

links the site of a hermitage on St Clement's Isle off the Cornish coast to the constellation Pleiades in its September position.

Other European investigators made their own studies of landmark alignments. Josef Heinsch, who worked in his native Germany and Czechoslovakia, discovered leys linking the sites of churches built on pre-Christian sites. More recently, in the early 1970s, the French investigator Lucien Richer discovered an extraordinary alignment of holy sites which spanned Europe from the island of Skerrig Michael off southwest Ireland to Mount Carmel in Israel, via St Michael's Mount in Cornwall, Mont St Michel in France,

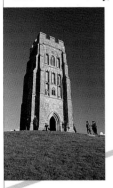

St Michael's tower on Glastonbury Tor.

and Delphi, Athens and Delos in Greece. On the ley are many of the important sanctuaries to St Michael, the standard bearer of the archangels, and Apollo, the Greek god of light. Most are sited on prominent outcrops.

ST MICHAEL'S LINE

As well as lying on the trans-European St Michael ley (see text, left), St Michael's Mount in Cornwall is at one end of the longest ley in Britain (see pictures opposite, left and below). This St Michael line coincides with the path of the rising sun on May Day and runs through the megalithic complex at Avebury, Wiltshire.

The medieval abbey at Bury St Edmunds, Suffolk, the eastern end of the St Michael line, described above.

DOWSING

Dowsing is the most popular form of divination in the West.

The traditional image of a dowser is of someone who is able to find underground water when its radiated energy, transmitted through a forked stick, causes a muscular reaction in the dowser's arms.

However, some dowsers believe that the movement of a dowsing rod or pendulum is caused by psychic rather than physical energy – that some "sixth sense" within

the dowser enables him or her to detect the energies emanating from the Earth.

Dowsers investigating earth energies claim to have discovered that ley lines and ancient sacred sites radiate powerful forces which can affect our wellbeing. They claim that ancient people were able to dowse in a totally natural manner and so built their sacred monuments at places where the earth energies were strongest. Dowsers may also use maps and diagrams to detect lost objects or to locate sickness in the body.

A dowser carries on the ancient divining tradition.

Neo-paganism and the New Age

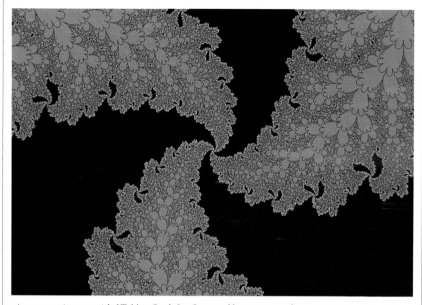

A computer image entitled Taking One's Leaf, *created by a program that generates iterative patterns from random starting-points. Such programs may be the closest science has come to replicating what many now believe to be the fundamental creative principle of the universe. Some neo-pagans use these images as mandalas, to aid meditation.*

In recent decades an increasing number of people in the West have come to view the ethical, political and economic basis of Western society as profoundly antipathetic to the physical and spiritual well-being of the world and its inhabitants. One product of this self-examination has been the growth since the 1960s of neo-paganism, a loose assemblage of new, eclectic belief systems based on reverence for the Earth and its natural cycles. Its foundations lie in 19th-century Romantic ideas of humankind living in harmony with nature, which inspired the revival of, for example, Druidism (see opposite page).

Many neo-pagan religions take as their starting-point an idealized Neolithic past in which human communities were more fully integrated with the natural world. According to this view, as the ancient Indo-Europeans migrated westwards, traditions based on reverence for the Earth (personified as the great mother goddess) and the cycles of nature were supplanted by a male-dominated, militaristic ethos expressed in a pantheon headed by wrathful sky gods. As a result, for several thousand years, people in the West lost sight of the importance of nature. So runs the most extreme and simplistic version of the theory.

In their search for a means of restoring this lost intimacy and establishing what they herald as a spiritual "New Age", neo-pagans look for inspiration to those peoples who keep shamanism alive, or to ancient cultures such as that of the Celts. The largest neo-pagan group, the Church of All Worlds, is based on veneration of a mother goddess. Another group, Feraferia, combines goddess worship with Greek polytheism.

Western followers of the Indian spiritual leader Sri Aurobindo (1872–1950) founded an experimental community named Auroville (below) near Pondicherry in southwest India in 1967, with the aim of demonstrating what he called "the conquest of life by the power of the spirit". They tried to show how people from all backgrounds and cultures could live in harmony.

DRUIDISM

According to Julius Caesar, the Celts possessed a revered élite, the Druids, who acted as priests and teachers and were the highest authority in all legal and spiritual matters. According to Irish sources of the 5th century AD, they were "men of art", religious specialists who travelled from tribe to tribe: they probably functioned as shamans. One aspect of druidic practice which struck early writers was the use of natural places of worship such as forest clearings or groves ("Druid" derives from the Greek for oak tree). One great sanctuary, on the isle of Anglesey, Wales, was devastated from the Romans in AD61.

In later centuries legends arose that Stonehenge and other Neolithic centres had been Druid temples. In fact, they are pre-Celtic, but the fallacy prompted the "revival" of druidic ceremonies, for example by the Order of Druids, founded in Wales in the late 19th century. Its members wear costumes inspired by ancient texts. Other groups have tried to revive a more accurate form of Celtic religion.

An architectural detail from Auroville, a spiritual community in India (see above).

Gardens of the spirit

A grand European garden design based loosely on the idea of an Indian Mughal palace: ambition and exoticism often combine in large-scale Western gardens.

More than 2,000 years ago King Darius the Great of Persia shut out the desert landscape with a garden running with fresh water and filled with trees, flowers and fruit as well as with exotic birds and animals. It was a paradise on Earth, a place of order and tranquillity redeemed from the wilderness. After the

The play of fountains in Islamic gardens had connotations of luxury (in a desert setting) and spiritual refreshment.

Arab conquest and the spread of Islam, the Persian gardens were destroyed, but the idea survived in Persian miniature paintings and woven garden carpets, thereby influencing the design of the sacred gardens that followed.

According to Marco Polo, who travelled the region in the late 13th century, Istawich, the ruler of the fortress of Alamut, had a garden that imitated the abode of the blessed in the *Koran*: it had pipes running with wine, milk, honey and water, and there were "fair ladies" in attendance – in keeping with the *Koran*'s four rivers of paradise and the black-eyed houris who care for the faithful through eternity.

Garden mazes have distant connotations of the spirit's quest for fulfilment.

In China, during the Han dynasty Emperor Wu is said to have created a lake garden, with islands that imitated the Mystic Isles, home of the Immortals. This model was highly influential in both China and Japan. Japanese gardens reflected a profound respect for nature, rooted in Shinto philosophy. Kami, the divine spirits of Shinto, were believed to be everywhere,

FINDHORN

In the early 1960s, in an attempt to ease the problem of their meagre income, a small group of people began to create a garden in the sand and gravel of a caravan park at Findhorn Bay on the Moray Firth in Scotland. Soon, one of their number, Dorothy Maclean, claimed to have made contact with what she described as "devas" or nature spirits.

Her first contact, the pea deva, allegedly told her that the garden would thrive if the group listened to the spirits of the plants and followed their advice about how to work the land. Within a few years, their efforts had produced cabbages weighing 40lb (18kg) and foxgloves more than 8 feet (2.5m) high.

The spectacle drew visitors from all over Britain, and before long, the world. Many of them were convinced that the crops proved the reality of nature spirits.

In the 1970s, Findhorn became a major inspiration for the emerging New Age movement.

---

populating all things in nature. The earliest shrines to Kami were clearings in a forest, each with one sacred tree, fenced in and covered with white pebbles, symbolizing an area set aside for the Kami to enter without being defiled. Over time, these shrines became more elaborate, sited in gardens that aimed to create the effect of an idealized landscape.

The profound respect for nature innate in Japanese culture is also evident in other garden styles. Zen Buddhist monks created dry gardens, or *karesansui*, as places for retreat and meditation. Relying on the placement of a few carefully chosen rocks, they are a meditation in themselves, expressing the essence of the landscape in a small space. Typically, the rocks are set in raked sand or gravel, whose wave-like patterns suggest water (see p.33). Raking the sand into precise configurations is used by the monks as a form of spiritual exercise.

The idea of spiritual refuge, where we can perceive a profound truth at the heart of nature, is central to many Western gardens too. The Romans built

The Indian painting A Flower From Every Meadow, *showing a garden used for ritual.*

grottoes dripping with water and dark with vegetation as homes of the nymphs, the spirits of nature. In medieval Europe, however, untamed nature was regarded as inimical, and so gardens were geometric, walled in like cloisters and filled with healing herbs as well as lilies, roses and other flowers with spiritual associations. The history of Western gardening in later periods has been one of restless negotiation with ideas of formality, wilderness and to *genius loci* ("the spirit of the place").

The Earth and the skies

The first recorded astronomers lived during the time of the earliest civilizations in Mesopotamia.

Some of these Old World stargazers may have been motivated by a religious or intellectual curiosity. However, in the New World, the texts and images of the Maya and Aztec civilizations certainly reveal that knowledge of the heavens and of complex and precise calendrical systems conferred a sacral status that was used to extend priestly power and social control.

The distinction between astrology and astronomy derives from the European scientific revolution of the 17th century. Astrology focused on the direct influence of the stars and planets on earthly events, whereas astronomy had an empirical basis. Before then, howev-

*An astronomer-astrologer. The two professions were rarely distinguished at this time (*c.*1500).*

*This circular structure, built by people of the pre-Inca Aymara culture (*c.*AD1000–1476), near Lake Titicaca in Bolivia, is claimed to be a sacred observatory used by priests of the cult of a sun god.*

Pre-Columbian rock drawings near Santa Fe, New Mexico, depicting spirit totems and the Dog Star, Sirius.

er, astral divination was an instrinsic part of the study of the heavens.

The Babylonians and other early civilizations of Mesopotamia placed great importance on the interpretation of omens, as we know from many inscribed clay tablets that have been discovered. The configuration resulting from molten lead when it was poured onto water, or the pattern of veins on the liver of a sacrificed beast, were taken as an indicator of the future, and a guide to conduct. In the same way, the behaviour of the stars and planets was full of significance for the conduct of our lives and of society.

The Babylonians are credited with having identified the Zodiac, a belt of twelve constellations through which the sun appeared to travel on its annual orbit of the Earth, and from this the Western and Hindu zodiacs were derived. Present-day Western astrology, however, has its roots specifically in the Greek system of nearly 2,000 years ago (the word "zodiac" itself comes from the Greek *zodiakos kyklos*, meaning "animal circle").

Scholars in both Babylon and Greece calculated the 18.6-year eclipse cycle with reasonable precision, but it was a Greek, in the 5th century BC, who first put forward a model of the solstice and equinox points, thus laying down the framework for an exact solar calendar.

The ability to locate the planets on the celestial sphere (that is, relative to the solstice and equinox points) was a great step forward, freeing scholars from the earlier reliance upon the four points of the compass, combined with the zenith (a point directly above) and

NAVAHO STARGAZERS

When Navaho people fall ill, they sometimes call on a stargazer to perform a curing ritual. The stargazer seeks to discover the cause of the sickness from the Holy People, supernatural beings who live in the skies. First he talks to the patient and his or her family and friends, and may chant or pray in the patient's hogan (dwelling). He may make a sandpainting, carefully outlining a sacred star and features of the land in white, blue, yellow and black powders. At some point in the ritual, the stargazer

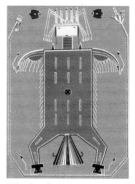

The thunder spirit represented in this Navaho sandpainting is believed to be responsible for what is called "male rain" – rain with thunder.

leaves the hogan and walks into the darkness carrying a quartz crystal. Alone, he chants and prays to a sacred being such as the Gila lizard, or to a star spirit, and then raises the crystal to the sky and gazes deeply into it, seeking out a bright star. When he sees strings of light streaming from the crystal, the stargazer has a vision of the cause of the illness, perhaps in the form of an animal or human or as lights of particular colours. The stargazer is able to use this inspiration from the Holy People to prescribe the rituals and medicine needed.

the nadir (a point directly below) as a framework for observation.

Because of the wobble of the Earth's axis over millennia, the signs of the zodiac no longer correspond with the constellations from which they take their name, and this discrepancy has led to many popular misconceptions.

Astrology is still the most popular form of divination in the West, in its

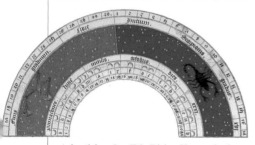

A detail from Les Très Riches Heures du duc de Berry, *15th century. Books of hours combine astronomical and liturgical information.*

"natal" (birth sign) manifestation (its "horary" manifestation interprets a situation of current alignments, at the time of seeking advice). However, the craft has lost status since the scientific revolution demolished the theory of geocentricity, according to which the sun moved around the Earth, the central point of the cosmos.

Theology was able to absorb the startling new cosmology, which to many (Newton included) revealed that God had created the heavens and the Earth according to principles more profoundly complex than people had hitherto suspected. However, astrology, which depended heavily on geocentricity, was less easily defended. In England, one founder member of the Royal Society (established 1662) denounced astrology as a "disgrace to reason", and later that century the government censored astrological publications (albeit on political as much as scientific grounds).

THE SOUTH AMERICAN SKIES

In the Inca worldview, as in other South American beliefs, astronomical phenomena are saturated with spiritual significance. This is reflected in part by the celestial character of major deities such as Inti (the sun god) and Mama Kilya (the moon goddess). However, the Milky Way was also seen as important, and the stars themselves were interpreted as minor deities.

Especially pre-eminent were the Pleiades, known as Collca (the "granary"), as they were the celestial protectors of agriculture and fertility. The star group known as Orqo-Cilay was believed to guard over royal llama flocks.

Central to Inca belief was the concept of *ceques*, or straight lines, radiating from the Sun Temple at the capital, Cuzco. Each was punctuated by a series of *huacas* (sacred sites), making sacred alignments. From Cuzco's central plaza the sunset on April 26 was observed between two pillars set on a peak to the west, and these pillars were themselves seen as a *huaca*. The *ceque* on which they were sited aligned (beyond the horizon) with a sacred spring named Catachillay – another name for the Pleiades. From the same square in Cuzco the setting Pleiades were observed earlier in the month.

The Incas attached importance to certain "dark cloud" constellations made up of dense clouds of stellar dust. Among them was the celestial Llama, which when it disappeared at midnight was thought to be drinking water from the Earth to prevent flooding.

Starry Night *(1899) by Vincent van Gogh. At the time he wrote, enigmatically, that life was probably "spherical and much more extensive than the hemisphere we know at present".*

Time chart

The interval between the development of modern humans *c*.100,000 years ago and the present day is a tiny fraction of the Earth's lifetime. But in that short time our influence on the planet has been profound: in the last 10,000 years alone agriculture and cities have transformed the landscape. The chart below plots the most significant strands of culture.

CULTURES AND SITES: NEAR EAST, ASIA, AFRICA AND OCEANIA

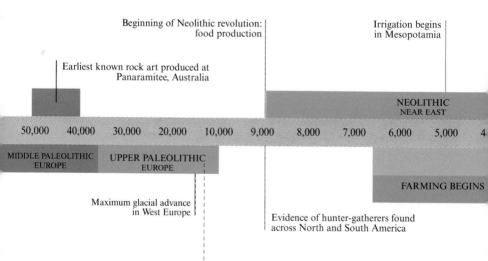

Beginning of Neolithic revolution: food production

Irrigation begins in Mesopotamia

Earliest known rock art produced at Panaramitee, Australia

NEOLITHIC NEAR EAST

| 50,000 | 40,000 | 30,000 | 20,000 | 10,000 | 9,000 | 8,000 | 7,000 | 6,000 | 5,000 | 4 |

MIDDLE PALEOLITHIC EUROPE

UPPER PALEOLITHIC EUROPE

FARMING BEGINS

Maximum glacial advance in West Europe

Evidence of hunter-gatherers found across North and South America

CULTURES AND SITES: EUROPE, NORTH AND SOUTH AMERICA

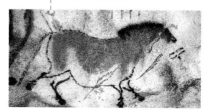

The cave paintings of Lascaux, southwestern France, c.15,000BC (see pp.98–9).

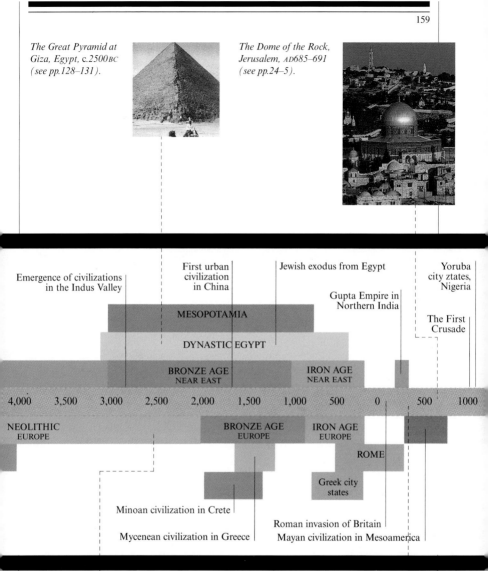

The Great Pyramid at Giza, Egypt, c.2500BC (see pp.128–131).

The Dome of the Rock, Jerusalem, AD685–691 (see pp.24–5).

Emergence of civilizations in the Indus Valley

First urban civilization in China

Jewish exodus from Egypt

Yoruba city ztates, Nigeria

Gupta Empire in Northern India

The First Crusade

| MESOPOTAMIA |
| DYNASTIC EGYPT |
| BRONZE AGE NEAR EAST | IRON AGE NEAR EAST |

| 4,000 | 3,500 | 3,000 | 2,500 | 2,000 | 1,500 | 1,000 | 500 | 0 | 500 | 1000 |

NEOLITHIC EUROPE	BRONZE AGE EUROPE	IRON AGE EUROPE
		ROME
		Greek city states

Minoan civilization in Crete

Mycenean civilization in Greece

Roman invasion of Britain

Mayan civilization in Mesoamerica

LEFT *Stonehenge, England, c.2500BC (see pp.122–3).*

RIGHT *Nazca lines, Peru, c.AD1-650 (see pp.108–9).*

Natural Phenomena

Earthquakes and tidal waves 1

The sheer scale of destruction caused by an earthquake can be awe-inspiring: a landscape unchanged in the history of a people may be broken up, lifted high above its accustomed level, or riven with cracks.

Striking suddenly with massive violence, earthquakes have often been attributed to divine agency, expressing the wrath of powerful gods. For example, for the Japanese, who inhabit an area of great seismic activity, tremors and quakes are traditionally said to be a manifestation of the storm god Susano. The ancient Greeks, who also lived in a region where earthquakes were (and still are) commonplace, believed them to be the work of the brother of Zeus, the sea and storm god Poseidon, to whom they sometimes gave the title Enosicthon ("Earth-shaker").

The most famous earthquake of classical mythology destroyed the civilization of Atlantis, a great continent which, according to Plato (*c.*427BC–347BC), existed far to the west beyond the Straits of Gibraltar, 9,000 years before his time. The civilization of Atlantis, whose rulers were of divine descent, flourished for centuries but then fell into moral decay, becoming strife-ridden and belligerent. The armies of Atlantis, Plato claimed, "came forth out of the Atlantic Ocean" and conquered much of Europe, North Africa and Asia. But then "there occurred violent earthquakes and floods" which consumed Atlantis "in one day and night of disaster".

Numerous theories, many of them fantastical, have been proposed to account for Atlantis as a place that in one form or another had real existence. However, the story is probably best seen as belonging to a whole group of myths, in many cultures, that relate the rise, flowering and decline of a world or race. Eventually the gods' anger at the degeneracy of the people can no longer be withheld, and the corruption is swept away in a divine cataclysm. In such stories earthquakes and other natural phenomena such as floods

Seismic disturbances occur frequently along the San Andreas Fault (opposite), a great crack in the Earth's crust where the Northern Pacific and North American tectonic plates slide against each other. The fault extends more than 500 miles (800km) along the western boundary of California: it is shown here as it cuts across the Carrizo Plain, 270 miles (432km) south of San Francisco. The city has been struck by several powerful earthquakes, most notably that of 1906 (see above and p.162).

Earthquakes and tidal waves 2

are frequent instruments of divine retribution.

Earthquakes, as omens, can also signify momentous change of a political or religious nature. The New Testament states that "the veil of the temple was rent ... and the earth did quake" at the moment of Christ's death on the cross (St Matthew, Ch.27).

As recently as 1819, the farmers of the Rann of Kutch, an area of irrigated coastal salt flats near the border of India and Pakistan, described a fault 10 feet (3m) high that

transience, the value of life.

The Earth's surface is in a permanent state of flux caused by the slow but constant movement of "tectonic plates", the individual sections that form the Earth's crust. According to the theory of "continental drift", first proposed by the German geophysicist Alfred Wegener (1880–1930) in 1912, there was originally one huge land mass or "supercontinent", which Wegener called Pangaea (All Earth). In the course of 200 million years,

ocean floor, or convergent (colliding so that one plate slides under another), characterized by "fold" mountain ranges where one plate has buckled under the pressure from another pushing against it.

It has been calculated that South America and Africa are drifting apart by two inches (5cm) every year, while the Pacific Ocean grows wider by half an inch (just over 1cm) every year.

Earthquakes occur when volcanoes erupt along fault lines or when adjacent

Earthquakes generally occur without warning and are over quickly: the quake which devastated San Francisco in 1906 (above) took place in the space of just 75 seconds, burying many as they slept.

Holes in the road appeared during a tremor which hit Los Angeles in 1971.

appeared after an earthquake in 1819 as Allah Bund (God's Dyke).

At a fundamental level, whatever our religious inclinations, earthquakes remind us of planetary perspectives on human life, the infinitesimal speck made by human history on the geophysical timescale. They also provide a focus for meditations on chance,

Pangaea broke into several pieces along great geological faults (lines of weakness in the Earth's crust where the inner molten core can break through), and its constituent components drifted apart. These faults are either divergent (pushing apart), characterized by deep trenches mainly in the

plates shift suddenly along part of the fault line that divides them. Most tremors are undetectable, but others cause widespread devastation, destroying human settlements, triggering avalanches, diverting rivers and creating crevasses and new faults in the Earth's surface.

One of the biggest

earthquakes in history occurred between Valdez and Anchorage, Alaska, in 1964. For some years, the convergent North Pacific and North American plates had become jammed in a zone more than 12 miles (20km) beneath Prince William Sound. Massive pressure built up around the jam until, on March 27, the pressure suddenly broke with an explosive force estimated as the equivalent of 200,000 megatons of TNT. The fastest shock waves travelled at more than 14,000mph

The 1989 San Francisco quake would have been more damaging but for strict post-1906 building laws.

(22,400kph). At Valdez, the docks fell into the sea and the water drained out of the harbour; mud, débris and people who were caught on the dockside were sucked down into a whirlpool which formed as a warehouse disappeared into the retreating water. Inland, the quake razed buildings over a wide area. In

Anchorage, one side of the main street collapsed, and the vibrations churned up deep subterranean clay supporting an entire residential neighbourhood, transforming the townscape into a mass of broken earth and collapsed homes which began to slip toward the sea. The upheavals in the land were huge: two children trying to flee were consumed by a deep fissure which opened in front of a house and then closed over them, and two people survived because they were standing on earth that rose 30 feet (9m) into the air when the rest of their neighbourhood collapsed.

The seismic shock waves from this earthquake also reverberated through the sea, setting in train a massive tidal wave, or *tsunami*, which caused destruction along the Pacific coast as far south as Crescent City, California, where seven people were killed.

A ship at sea near the epicentre of an earthquake may experience little more than a sharp jolt, because the most powerful shock waves are far below the surface of the water. The deep ocean presents little resistance to seismic waves, which may travel thousands of miles without diminishing in power (South American quakes have affected New Zealand,

Japan and Hawaii). As they approach land, they encounter greater resistance in the shallows and slow down abruptly, but their tremendous momentum causes water to pile up to a great height: in 1993, a *tsunami* in the Sea of Japan rose nearly 100 feet (30m) above sea-level. The *tsunami* that struck the tip of the Kamchatka peninsula in Siberia in 1737 was 230 feet (70m) high.

Like earthquakes, *tsunamis* may also be triggered by a volcanic eruption. When the island

A steamship struck by a tidal wave in the West Indies in 1867.

of Krakatoa, to the west (not the east, as Hollywood would have it) of Java, blew up in August 1883, the explosion was heard 2,500 miles (4,000km) away and set off a *tsunami* 115 feet (35m) high that devastated low-lying islands and coastal communities along the Sunda Strait, including one village 10 miles (16km) inland.

Thunder and lightning

In many cultures thunderstorms have been associated with powerful male warrior divinities. For example, among the Yoruba of West Africa it is said that the great god of thunder, Shango, was the greatest of the Yoruba warrior-monarchs. Farther east, in Rwanda, the supreme lord of heaven is Lightning, Nkuba. According to Hindu myth, thunder and lightning are the weapons of the warrior god Indra, the chief of the Vedic (early Hindu) pantheon who was known as *Vajri* (Wielder of

Hephaistos (Vulcan) by the Cyclopes. One myth relates how Zeus used a thunderbolt to kill Asklepios, the demi-god of healing, because he raised a man from the dead; in revenge the god Apollo killed the Cyclopes.

In pagan Germanic myth, thunderstorms and associated phenomena were the province of a mighty sky god, Donar ("Thunder"), later called Thunor by the Anglo-Saxons and Thor in Scandinavia. In his celestial battles against dragons and giants, Thor wielded a

widely envisaged as a great bird, the Thunderbird, which resembles a giant eagle (in the northwest coastal region it is said to be able to carry off whales). Lightning is caused by the flashing of the Thunderbird's eyes, thunder by the beating of its wings. Like other thunder deities, the beast is fierce but also a protector of humanity against evil forces: just as Thor was said to have fought malevolent giants, in some areas of North America thunderstorms were believed to be the

Before a storm, cumulus clouds grow dark as the density of moisture increases.

Rain, ice and winds generate electrical explosions seen as lightning and heard as thunderclaps. As light travels faster than sound, lightning is usually seen a few seconds before thunder is heard.

the Thunderbolt); the sacred text *Rig Veda* describes how he used his thunderbolts to kill the dragon Vritra.

Similarly, thunderbolts were said to be the main weapons of Zeus (Jupiter), the supreme god of the Greco-Roman pantheon, for whom they were made in the underground forges of the smith-god

hammer-axe, the blows of which caused thunder and lightning; his red beard was also a symbol of lightning. The god was equated with the thunderbolt-hurling Jupiter or Jove, and hence gave his name to Thursday (Latin: *Jovis dies,* "Jove's day").

In Native North American myth the spirit of thunder and lightning is

Thunderbird's battles against malign underworld beings.

Western scientists began to understand thunderstorms in the 18th century. In 1752, Benjamin Franklin in the USA and M. d'Alibard in France, working independently, flew kites in storms and demonstrated that thunder and lightning were electrical phenomena. Within a raincloud, warm, moist air rises, sometimes at more than 80mph (128 kph). High in the clouds the air condenses, freezes, and falls to earth as hail; in the lower reaches of the cloud, the hail melts and turns to rain. But as the prevailing winds grow stronger, the rain or hail may be blown up again with violence, freezing rapidly to create hailstones that may be as much as 3 inches (7.5cm) across, falling at 60mph (96kph). This process generates vast

A bolt of lightning generated by a waterspout "twister" near Lake Okeechobee, Florida.

amounts of electricity, giving the cloud an electrical charge. In a process not yet fully understood, this is released as lightning, a huge, negatively charged spark which seeks a positive contact, in the cloud, in another cloud, or, most destructively, on the ground.

In 55BC the Roman author Lucretius proposed that thunder was the crashing of clouds, but modern science suggests that it is caused by the sudden, massive expansion of the air in the path of a lightning bolt.

A single bolt may be several miles long. It is common to distinguish forked lightning from sheet lightning, but the sheet effect is simply the result of the bolt being obscured by clouds. The human eye can only detect a single flash of lightning, but high-speed photography has shown that a bolt in fact consists of a series of rapid descending and ascending strokes which occur in the space of a few thousandths of a second. Lightning is most common in thunderstorms, but it can also accompany snowstorms, sandstorms, tornadoes and waterspouts. It has even been reported in clear air: a literal "bolt from the blue".

Ash, pumice and other material ejected from erupting volcanoes also generate enough electrical energy to cause lightning. When submarine volcanic eruptions created the island of Surtsey south of Iceland in November 1963, violent explosions hurled massive clouds of ash high into the sky at 200mph (320kph). These eruptions sometimes blazed with short, zig-zag bursts of lightning.

Lightning is also manifested as red, orange or yellow balls of electricity lasting for a few seconds, which have been seen hanging in mid-air or falling from clouds to the ground, sometimes bouncing when they make contact. These bolts are often accompanied by peculiar sounds and smells. In 1936 it was reported in Britain that a red ball struck a house, cut the telephone wire, burnt the window frame and fell into a bowl of water, causing it to come to the boil. According to one

Lightning diffused, obscured or reflected by clouds appears as "sheet lightning".

theory, the location of some prehistoric stone circles in Britain and elsewhere may have been influenced by sightings of ball lightning. For example, it has been reported over Avebury in southwest England (see pp.120–21). At such places the phenomenon may be connected with the local topography, geology or geomagnetism.

Hurricanes and floods

Storms and floods are the most commonplace of all natural disasters, and feature prominently in the mythology of peoples on every continent.

The word "hurricane" comes from Mesoamerican myth: the name of the Quiché Maya storm god, Huracán, was adopted into Spanish as the word for a great storm, and passed thence into many other European languages (English *hurricane*, French *ouragan*, German *Orkan,* and so on).

Storm divinities such as

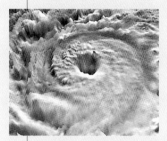

A computer-enhanced view of a hurricane off the Gulf of Mexico in 1980: its eye is clearly visible.

the Greek Poseidon and the Japanese Susano are figures of awesome power who embody the forces of disorder and turmoil. However, as controllers of the rains they may also be bringers of fertility; an example of this dual role is the ancient Canaanite storm god Baal.

In myth, floods may appear as disasters of cosmic proportions which wipe out the human race, often because a divinity chooses to punish people for their transgressions. In the Jewish and Christian traditions, the most famous flood narrative is the Biblical story of Noah. The account in Genesis probably derives from the deluge myths of the ancient civilizations of southern Mesopotamia, a region prone to serious flooding, where the great rivers Tigris and Euphrates meet. There are striking parallels in these accounts: the flood, caused by rainstorms, is divinely decreed to punish sinful humans, but one man – Noah in the Hebrew Scriptures; Atrahasis (see p.15), Utnapishtim and Ziusudra in the three older accounts that are extant – survives the disaster by building a ship and, after the waters have receded, begins the repopulation of the world.

The Middle Eastern stories may have influenced the Greek myth of Deucalion, the son of Prometheus, and his wife Pyrrha, who were the sole survivors of a cosmic deluge sent by the god Zeus. They may also have some connection with the Indian myth of Manu, the first man, who was forewarned by a great fish of an imminent cataclysmic

storm and flood and survived by constructing a boat. But such stories are common anywhere that is prone to floods. For example, one southern Chinese myth recounts how two children, a brother and sister, survived a flood caused by the Thunder God by floating on the floodwaters inside a great gourd. They later married and repopulated the world.

The idea of a new cosmos emerging after the destruction of the old by storm and flood is not confined to the Old World:

Motorists dodge power lines felled by Hurricane Alicia, which hit Texas in 1983.

according to the Aztec myth of the Five Suns (worlds), the second Sun ended when its presiding deity, Quetzalcoatl, was carried off by a hurricane. The present, fifth, Sun arose after the fourth was annihilated by a flood and the people turned into fish.

In some cultures the flood may be caused by the misdemeanour of an individual. For example, the Chewong people of Malaya believe that disastrous inundations occur if a person mocks an animal, thereby provoking the anger of the primal underworld serpent, the controller of the floodwaters. The Aboriginal mythology of northern Australia also includes numerous origin myths in which a great serpent identified or associated with the rainbow causes a storm and flood after being angered by an ancestral hero or heroine. The flood

In the West storms were seen as the work of the Devil, who is seen here on the church steeple in a woodcut of 1613.

sweeps away the previous society and landscape. It is believed that such myths may well be rooted in the rise in sea-levels after the last ice age.

Storms and hurricanes arise from the movements within the Earth's atmosphere as the sun heats its surface, causing wind as hot air rises and cooler air sinks. Some of the strongest winds are generated in association with cyclones – powerful rotating wind systems. Cyclones occur worldwide but are particularly prominent in tropical regions during late summer and autumn, when very warm and moist areas of high pressure run into cold low pressure areas coming from the north or south. At the point of collision between the two air masses, the Coriolis effect (a spinning motion caused by the rotation of the Earth) causes a cyclone. Cyclonic winds circulate anti-clockwise in the northern hemisphere and clockwise in the southern hemisphere.

The lower the pressure at the centre of the cyclone, the stronger the winds swirling into it. Around the focal point of the cyclone, a calm and cloudless low pressure area known as the "eye", the rotating winds are at their fiercest, forming a spinning cylinder of wind known as the "eye wall". The combination of violent rising winds and great humidity engenders the dense raincloud formation and precipitation that are characteristic of cyclonic systems.

A severe cyclone containing winds of at least 75mph (120kph) is described by various names, depending on location: in the Atlantic, the Caribbean and Gulf of Mexico it is called a hurricane, in the Indian Ocean a cyclone, and in the China Sea and western Pacific a typhoon.

These giant swirling storms may be up to 1,200 miles (1,920km) wide, with winds averaging more than 100mph (160kph). In the strongest storms, sustained gusts may even exceed a highly destructive 200mph (320kph). Tornadoes may also accompany a hurricane (see pp.168–9).

When the eye of a hurricane, usually around 20–25 miles (30–40km) in diameter, passes over, the violent winds and rain cease temporarily – only to return with equal force when the other side of the eye wall strikes.

Bangladesh is particularly vulnerable to cyclones from the Bay of Bengal, as most of the country is less than 52 feet (16m) above sea-level. The worst destruction is the result of the "tidal surge" that is caused by fierce winds whipping up the sea to many feet above its normal level. On November 12 and 13, 1970, a devastating cyclone brought winds of over 150mph (240kph) and caused a tidal surge with waves up to 23 feet (7m) high. At least 300,000 people perished.

Tornadoes, whirlwinds and whirlpools

One of the most awe-inspiring of the Earth's meteorological phenomena is the vortex: a tight, rotating funnel of water or wind.

In large bodies of water a vortex may form as a whirlpool, which develops when currents collide at sea, sometimes resulting in great swirling eddies or a *maelstrom* (from the Dutch, "whirling stream") – a giant whirlpool capable of sucking ships into the depths of the sea. In Greek myth this phenomenon is represented by the female terrifying whirlpool with enough force to swallow any ships nearby. The hero Odysseus survived an encounter with Charybdis by clinging to the branch of a tree as his ship disappeared into the vortex.

Whirlpools pose a regular threat to ships in several areas, such as the Naruto Strait (between the Sea of Japan and the Pacific), the Hebrides and Orkney Islands (Scotland) and the Lofoten islands (off northern Norway). In the Lofotens, the treacherous Norwegian maelstrom has to flow around an obstacle. This movement creates a twisting column of air that develops a downdraft in the centre. As the whirlwind moves, it picks up dirt and litter and becomes visible as a cloud of dust, from 3 feet (1m) to several hundred feet high. Such whirlwinds are especially common in dry seasons in tropical regions during the heat of the day. They range from "dust devils" and other relatively gentle eddies to towering tornadoes of immense destructive power. Dust

The aftermath of a tornado, Miami, Florida, 1926. While they generally claim fewer victims than hurricanes, on a local level tornadoes are the most destructive of all meteorological phenomena.

Tornadoes form beneath storm clouds, extending toward the ground as they gather force.

monster Charybdis, the offspring of the Earth goddess Gaia and the sea god Poseidon. Charybdis, said to inhabit the Strait of Messina between Sicily and mainland Italy, sucked in water three times a day in a moves between the islands of Moskenesøya and Mosken in a band about five miles (8km) wide.

Vortices in the air arise as a result of the Coriolis effect (see p.167), and the process of their formation is similar to that of the biggest storms and hurricanes. Heated surface air rises and may begin to spiral, especially when it devils are small whirlwinds that occur where the temperature of the Earth's surface is high, as in tropical regions.

A tornado (from the Spanish *tronado*, "thunderstorm") forms beneath a thundercloud, in areas where high humidity combines with zones of warm and cool air. A fast, narrow updraft of air rises from the Earth's warm surface into a thundercloud where the temperature may be at 32°F (0°C). The Coriolis effect causes the updraft to spin, eventually giving rise to the characteristic funnel-shaped "twister". A tornado can also develop when a dust devil contacts a developing cumulus cloud overhead.

The conditions in which tornadoes form are typical of the northern hemisphere spring in general, and of the midwestern United States, northern India, northern Indochina and

Waterspouts are less powerful than land tornadoes owing to their heavy burden of water.

China in particular. Smaller tornadoes also occur in southern Britain and mainland western Europe. Many tornadoes peter out before they develop fully, and about two-thirds of them exist for no more than three minutes.

When a tornado funnel touches ground it sucks most things in its path into the sky and scatters débris

from its base. The funnel may be 800–2,000 feet (250–600m) high, with a base measuring from 300–1,000 feet (100–300m) in diameter.

The whole funnel moves across the landscape at an average speed of just 30–40mph (50–70kph), but the winds within the vortex reach at least 300mph (500kph), and sometimes even the speed of sound (approximately 750mph/ 1,200kph). However, the exact speed of the spinning winds inside a tornado can only be estimated, as few meteorological measuring instruments will withstand a twister's onslaught.

Witnesses describe the noise of a tornado as resembling a giant swarm of bees or the roaring of jet engines. The few who have lived to tell of the interior of a tornado describe a whirling mass sparking constantly with lightning. The air pressure in the middle of the vortex is extremely low: buildings may explode with the sudden drop in pressure when a tornado strikes.

Twisters have been known to lift trains off railroad tracks and to move entire houses some distance and set them down again. A tornado will also suck up water and fish from rivers and deposit them elsewhere.

The worst tornado on record touched down in

Missouri on March 18, 1925, and travelled for 200 miles (350km) through Missouri, Illinois and Indiana, destroying towns and leaving 689 people dead. The twister's parent cloud was so close to the ground that the funnel was not visible: one eyewitness described it as a strange fog rolling toward him under a boiling mass of cloud.

Tornadoes in mountain regions ("mountainadoes") form when small vortices are magnified as they come into contact with cooler air flowing across the

A "twister" careers between pylons in East St Louis, Illinois, in 1990. The mid-western USA experiences frequent tornadoes as hot air from the Gulf of Mexico meets cooler westerlies coming down from the Rockies.

mountains. During one winter in Boulder, Colorado, a storm of mountainadoes developed, each a huge spinning mass of snow about 100 feet (30m) across, generating winds of 90mph (150kph).

Glossary

Akkadians a Semitic people who were established in northern Sumer (in Mesopotamia) by the middle of the 3rd millennium BC and subsequently occupied the whole of Sumer.

Algonkians speakers of the Algonkian group of Native American languages; most live in the boreal forests of northeastern North America.

Anatolia a mountainous region of Asian Turkey, which had important towns, such as Çatal Hüyük, in the Neolithic period.

Animism the belief, especially in various non-Western cultures, that all objects, animate and inanimate, possess a living spirit essence.

Ashtoreth an ancient Near Eastern mother goddess, worshipped as a fertility deity; her cult spread from Phoenicia throughout the Mediterranean.

Assyria an empire in northern Mesopotamia that began to expand *c.*1300BC and at its height reached Egypt and the Mediterranean; the Assyrian empire fell in 612BC.

Babylonia the region of southern Mesopotamia, including Sumer and Akkad, of which Babylon was the chief city between *c.*1850BC and *c.*300BC.

Barrows earthen burial mounds constructed in a wide variety of shapes and sizes; their inner architecture often consists of stone passages and chambers.

Brigid an Irish goddess associated with fertility, agriculture and creativity; in the early years of Christianity she was adopted as St Bride or Bridget, patroness of Ireland.

Bronze Age the period in which bronze was the primary material used to make tools and weapons (in Asia during the 3rd and 2nd millennia BC and in Europe during the 2nd and early 1st millennia BC).

Ceques in Inca belief, sacred straight "lines" radiating from the Sun Temple at Cuzco, along which *huacas* (q.v.) were found.

Cheyenne a native people of the western Great Plains of North America.

Chippewa an alternative name for the Ojibwa people of North America.

Choctaw a native people of the western Great Plains of North America.

Comanche a native people of the southeastern Great Plains of North America.

Crow a native people of western North America.

Culture hero a heroic, generally legendary, figure who performs extraordinary feats in the course of laying the foundations of a society.

Cybele an Anatolian mother goddess whose cult spread throughout the Roman Empire after 204BC, when her statue was brought to Rome; she was celebrated in fertility rites at the spring equinox.

Demeter an ancient Greek nature goddess, responsible for the fruitfulness of the earth, and agriculture; she and her daughter Persephone were worshipped as grain goddesses, representing new growth (Persephone) and the harvest (Demeter).

Devi "the Goddess", the supreme female deity of Hinduism; her many aspects function as discrete goddesses, such as Parvati, the wife of Shiva, and the fierce and terrible Kali (q.v.).

Gaia in Greek mythology, the primal goddess embodying the Earth, the mother of Uranus, the Heavens, and Pontus, the Sea; she was the original goddess of the landscape and nature.

Ganga in Hindu mythology, the divine personification of the river Ganges; she is associated with health and abundance, and her sacred water is believed to wash away sins.

Ishtar in Babylonian and Assyrian mythology, the goddess of love, sexuality and fertility; associated with many earth goddesses, including Ashtoreth, she was responsible for the fertility of nature and humanity.

Hittites a people who appeared in what are now Turkey and northern Syria during the 2nd millennium BC; they produced the earliest known Indo-European writing. The Hittites built up a great empire which collapsed *c.*1200BC.

Hogan a traditional Navaho dwelling, made of mud supported by wooden timbers.

Huaca in Inca belief, a feature of the landscape imbued with mythic significance and supernatural power.

Isis in Egyptian mythology, an earth and fertility goddess, the sister and wife of Osiris.

Kali in Hindu mythology, the great warrior goddess and enemy of demons; usually represented with symbols of life (such as food bowls or the lotus) and death (such as a necklace of weapons or severed heads).

Khnum in Egyptian myth, a creator god worshipped into

the early New Kingdom period; he was said to have fashioned people and deities on a potter's wheel.

Luiseño a Native American people of the southern coast of what is now California.

Manitou an Algonkian (q.v.) term describing the all-pervading divine spirit.

Medicine wheel a prehistoric arrangement of stones and boulders found on the North American plains and prairies that resembles a wheel, with an outer "rim" and radiating "spokes".

Megalith any prehistoric, massive block of stone of the kind widely erected in northwest Europe from c.3200–c.1500BC.

Mesopotamia the region, now largely in Iraq, between and adjacent to the rivers Tigris and Euphrates, where the Sumerian, Akkadian, Babylonian and Assyrian civilizations developed.

Navaho the most numerous of the Native American peoples; they live mainly in Arizona and northern New Mexico.

Neolithic the last period of the Stone Age. It lasted in Europe from about 6,000 to 4,500 years ago and in southwest Asia from about 11,000 to 8,000 years ago. The earliest organized agriculture dates from this period.

Ojibwa an Algonkian people of the Great Lakes region of North America; they are also called the Chippewa.

Paleolithic Age literally "Old Stone Age". The period characterized by the use of rudimentary chipped stone tools, from 2.5 million years ago until the beginning of the Mesolithic period ("Middle Stone Age"), c.8500BC. The Middle Paleolithic began approximately 200,000 years ago; the Upper Paleolithic, 35,000 years ago.

Pediment the triangular end of the pitched roof of a Greek temple or other building.

Pegmatite a rock with very large, interlocking crystals.

Phoenicians a Semitic seafaring people of the ancient eastern Mediterranean coast (approximately present-day Lebanon and northern Israel). Great Phoenician cities included Sidon, Tyre, Berytus (Beirut), which were conquered by Alexander the Great and later the Romans, who also destroyed a Phoenician empire based on Carthage in North Africa.

Pueblo any of the native peoples of southwestern North America who traditionally live in settled agricultural towns or villages (*pueblos* in Spanish); they include the Hopi and Zuñi.

Sami or Saami a Finno-Ugric people, known to outsiders as the Lapps, of northern Scandinavia and the far northeast of Russia.

Shaman a ritual specialist who contacts the spirits and communes with them in order to cure, divine or send magical illness; an important figure in the tribal societies of Asia, the Americas and parts of Africa.

Shiva in Hindu mythology, a great god of nature and fertility who embodies the contrary forces of destruction and rebirth; as he represents male creative energy, his symbol is the lingam, or erect phallus.

Sumerians a non-Semitic people who established a civilization in Sumer (also called Sumeria) in southern Mesopotamia during the 4th millennium BC and developed the first writing, cities and law codes; they were superseded by the Akkadians.

Ta'aroa in Tahitian mythology, the creator god who fashioned human beings and provided the island's staple foodstuff, breadfruit.

Tiamat in Akkadian mythology, the primal female monster who gave birth to the gods; she was slain by the god Marduk, who cut her in two; one half of her body became the sky and the other the earth.

Trickster a figure found in myth and folklore all over the world. He may be human, animal or divine. Mischievously, he subverts the activities of humans and gods alike. Examples are Raven and Coyote in Native North America, Loki in Scandinavian myth.

Vision quest the induction of an ecstatic state of spiritual enlightenment through a regime of fasting, prayer and seclusion.

Yggdrasil in Scandinavian mythology, a mighty tree, also known as the World Ash, that forms the axis of the world.

Yin and Yang in Chinese thought, the female-male principle of the balanced complementariness of opposites.

Ymir a primeval giant of Scandinavian myth. Created from ice, he was killed by the god Odin and his two brothers, who formed the earth from his body, the seas from his blood, the sky from his skull.

Ziggurat a pyramidal Babylonian temple-tower consisting of a number of storeys, each one smaller than the one below it.

Zuñi a Pueblo people of New Mexico in southwestern North America.

Bibliography

Albanese, C.L. *Nature Religion in America from the Algonkian Indians to the New Age* University of Chicago Press, Chicago, Illinois, and London, 1990

Allen, J. and Griffiths, J. *The Book of the Dragon* Charwell Books, Secaucus, New Jersey/Orbis Publishing, London, 1979

Ashe, G. *Mythology of the British Isles* Methuen, London/Trafalgar Square Publishing, North Pomfret, Vermont, 1990

Aveni, A. (ed.) *Native American Astronomy* University of Texas Press, Austin, Texas, and London, 1977

Aveni, A.F. (ed.) *World Archaeoastronomy* Cambridge University Press, Cambridge, England, and New York, 1989

Balmuth, M.S. and Rowland, R.J. (eds.) *Studies in Sardinian Archaeology* University of Michigan Press, Ann Arbor, Michigan, 1984

Barrett, W. and Besterman, T. *The Divining Rod* University Books, New York, 1968

Bierhorst, J. *The Mythology of North America* William Morrow, New York, 1985

Bierhorst, J. *The Mythology of South America* William Morrow, New York, 1988

Bierhorst, J. *The Mythology of Mexico and Central America* William Morrow, New York, 1990

Broder, P.J. *Hopi Painting* E.P. Dutton, New York, 1978

Bruce-Mitford, R. *The Sutton Hoo Ship Burial, a Handbook* (3rd edn) British Museum Publications, London, 1979

Bullard, F.M. *Volcanoes of the Earth* (revised edn) University of Texas Press, Austin, Texas, and London, 1976

Burl, A. *The Stone Circles of the British Isles* Yale University Press, New Haven, Connecticut, and London, 1976

Burl, A. *From Carnac to Callanish* Yale University Press, New Haven, Connecticut, and London, 1993

Carrasco, D. (ed.) *To Change Place, Aztec Ceremonial Landscapes* University Press of Colorado, Niwot, Colorado, 1991

Castleden, R. *Neolithic Britain* Routledge, London and New York, 1992

Chippindale, C. *Stonehenge Complete* Thames and Hudson, London/Cornell University Press, Ithaca, New York, 1983

Coudert, A. *Alchemy: the Philosopher's Stone* Wildwood, London/Shambhala Publications, Boulder, Colorado, 1980

Cunliffe, B. *The City of Bath* Yale University Press, New Haven, Connecticut, and London, 1986

Dames, M. *The Silbury Treasure* Thames and Hudson, London and New York, 1976

Eiby, G.A. *Earthquakes* Heinemann Educational, London/Van Nostrand Reinhold, New York, 1980

Etienne, R. *Pompeii, The Day a City Died* (Palmer, C., trans.) Harry N. Abrams, New York/Thames and Hudson, London, 1992

Fakhry, A. *The Pyramids* (2nd edn) University of Chicago Press, Chicago and London, 1969

Fontenrose, J. *The Delphic Oracle* University of California Press, Berkeley, California, and London, 1978

Gasparini, G. and Margolies, L. *Inca Architecture* (Lyon, P. trans.) Indiana University Press, Bloomington, Indiana, and London, 1980

Godwin, J. *Mystery Religions in the Ancient World* Harper and Row, San Francisco/Thames and Hudson, London, 1981

Grant, C. *Canyon de Chelly, Its People and Rock Art* University of Arizona Press, Tucson, Arizona, 1978

Griffin-Pierce, T. *Earth is My Mother, Sky is My Father: Space, Time and Astronomy in Navajo Sandpainting* University of New Mexico Press, Albuquerque, 1992

Hadingham, E. *Lines to the Mountain Gods, Nazca and the Mysteries of Peru* Harrap, London/Random House, New York, 1987

Halifax, J. *Shaman, the Wounded Healer* Thames and Hudson, London and New York, 1982

Hawkes, J. *Atlas of Ancient Archaeology* McGraw Hill, New York

Hemming, J. and Ranney, E. *Monuments of the Incas* Little, Brown & Co, Boston, 1982

Hultkrantz, A. *The Religions of the American Indians* (Setterwall, M., trans.) University of California Press, Berkeley, California, and London, 1979

Isaacs, J. *Arts of the Dreaming, Australia's Living Heritage* Lansdowne, Sydney, 1984

Joralemon, D. and Douglas, S. *Sorcery and Shamanism, Curanderos and Clients in Northern Peru* University of Utah Press, Salt Lake City, Utah, 1993

Joussaume, R. *Dolmens for the Dead* (Chippindale A. and C., trans.) Batsford, London, 1987/Cornell University Press, Ithaca, New York, 1988

Kehoe, T.F. *Indian Boulder Effigies* Saskatchewan Museum of Natural History Popular Series 12, Regina, Saskatchewan, 1965

Korp, M. *The Sacred Geography of the American Mound Builders* Edwin Mellen Press, Lewiston, New York, and Lampeter, Wales, 1990

Kruger, C. (ed.) *Volcanoes* G.P. Putnam's Sons, New York, 1971

Laporte, D.G. *Christo* (Pollak, A., trans.) Pantheon, New York, 1986

Laude, J. *African Art of the Dogon, the Myths of the Cliff Dwellers* (Neugroschel, J., trans.) The Brooklyn Museum and Viking Press, New York, 1973

Layton, R. *Australian Rock Art* Cambridge University Press, Cambridge and New York, 1992

Leach, M. and Fried, J. (eds.) *Standard Dictionary of Folklore, Mythology and Legend* Funk and Wagnalls, New York, 1972

Loewe, M. and Blacker, C. *Oracles and Divination* Shambhala Publications, Boulder, Colorado/Allen and Unwin, London, 1981

Lurker, M. *The Gods and Symbols of Ancient Egypt, an Illustrated Dictionary* (Cummings, B., trans.) Thames and Hudson, London and New York, 1980

Mallam, R.C. *The Iowa Effigy Mound Manifestation: an Interpretative Model* Office of the State Archaeologist Report 9, University of Iowa, Iowa City, Iowa, 1976

Manley, J. *Atlas of Prehistoric Britain* Phaidon Press, Oxford/Oxford University Press, New York, 1989

McGaa, E. *Mother Earth Spirituality* Harper and Row, San Francisco and London, 1990

Meletzis, S and Papadakis, H. *Delphi, Sanctuary and Museum* (Freeson, R.C. trans.) Schnell and Steiner, Munich /Argonaut, Chicago, 1967

Melton, J.G., Clark, J. and Kelly, A. *New Age Encyclopedia* Gale Research, Detroit, Michigan and London, 1990

Michell, J. *The New View Over Atlantis* Thames and Hudson, London, 1983

Michell, J. *The Earth Spirit* Thames and Hudson, New York, 1975

Moon, B. (ed.) *An Encyclopedia of Archetypal Symbolism* Shambhala Publications, Boston, Massachusetts and London, 1991

Morphy, H. (ed.) *Animals Into Art* Unwin Hyman, London and Boston, 1989

Nance, J.J. *On Shaky Ground* William Morrow, New York, 1988

O'Kelly, M.J. *Early Ireland* Cambridge University Press, Cambridge and New York, 1989

Peterson, N. (ed.) *Tribes and Boundaries in Australia* Australian Institute of Aboriginal Studies, Canberra/Humanities Press, New Jersey, 1976

Piggot, S. *The Druids* Thames and Hudson, London, 1985

Powers, W.K. *Oglala Religion* University of Nebraska Press, Lincoln, Nebraska, and London, 1975

Ritchie, D. *The Ring of Fire* Atheneum, New York, 1981

Rodley, L. *Cave Monasteries of Byzantine Cappadocia* Cambridge University Press, Cambridge and New York, 1985

Rose, D. B. *Dingo Makes Us Human* Cambridge University Press, Cambridge and New York, 1992

Ruspoli, M. *The Cave of Lascaux* (Wormell, S., trans.) Thames and Hudson, London/Harry N. Abrams, New York, 1987

Scully, V. *The Earth, the Temple and the Gods, Greek Sacred Architecture* (revised ed.) Yale University Press, New Haven, Connecticut, and London, 1979

Silverberg, R. *Mound Builders of Ancient America* New York Graphic Society, Greenwich, Connecticut, 1968

Stockel, H.H. *Survival of the Spirit, Chiricahua Apaches in Captivity* University of Nevada Press, Reno, Nevada, and London, 1993

Sullivan, M. *The Cave Temples of Maichishan* University of California Press, Berkeley, California, 1969

Thacker, C. *The History of Gardens* Croom Helm, London/University of California Press, Berkeley, California, 1979

Townsend, R.F. (ed.) *The Ancient Americas, Art from Sacred Landscapes* The Art Institute of Chicago, Chicago/Prestel Verlag, Munich, 1992

Ucko, P.J. and Rosenfeld, A. *Palaeolithic Cave Art* Weidenfeld & Nicolson, London, 1987

Ucko, P.J. (ed.) *Form in Indigenous Art* Duckworth, London/Humanities Press, New Jersey, 1977

Ucko, P.J., Hunter, M., Clark and A.J., David, A. *Avebury Reconsidered From the 1660s to the 1990s* Unwin Hyman, London and Boston, Massachusetts, 1991

Welch, S.C. *Persian Painting* George Braziller, New York, 1976

Wenkam, R. *The Edge of Fire* Sierra Club Books, San Francisco, 1987

Whitehose, R.D. (ed.) *Dictionary of Archaeology* Macmillan, London/Facts on File Publications, New York, 1983

Willcox, A.R. *The Rock Art of Africa* Croom Helm, London/Holmes and Meier, New York, 1984

Williams, N.M. *The Yolngu and their Land* Australian Institute of Aboriginal Studies, Canberra/Stanford University Press, Stanford, 1986

Willis, R.G. (gen. ed.) *World Mythology* Simon and Schuster, London/Holt, New York, 1993

Willis, R.G. (ed.) *Signifying Animals, Human Meaning in the Natural World* Unwin Hyman, London and Boston, 1990

Index

Page numbers indicate a reference in the main text. There may be references in captions or feature boxes on the same page. Page numbers in *italic* indicate a reference in an illustration caption only. Page numbers in **bold** indicate a reference in a feature box.

Photo Credits

The publisher thanks the photographers and organizations for their kind permission to reproduce the following photographs in this book:

Abbreviations
B below; C centre; T top; L left; R right
BAL: Bridgeman Art Library
DBP: Duncan Baird Publishers
FLPA: Frank Lane Picture Agency
ESA: European Space Agency
HPL: Hutchison Picture Library
MEPL: Mary Evans Picture Library
PLI: Picture Library International
RHPL: Robert Harding Picture Library
SPL: Science Photo Library
WFA: Werner Forman Archive

1 Zefa; 2 Zefa; 6 RHPL; 8/9 Zefa; 10 ESA/ PLI/SPL; 11T Zefa; 11BL Wheelwright Museum of the American Indian; 11BR RHPL/Woolfitt; 12 K. Wilks; 13 BAL/British Library; 14T Frank Spooner Pictures/Lewis; Zefa/Sunak; 14B DBP; 16 WFA/Private Collection; 17T James Pierce; 17B BAL/Ali Meyer; 18B Zefa/Sunak; 18/19 BAL/British Museum; 19B BAL/Phillips; 20 Biblioteca Apostolica Vaticana; 21B MEPL; 21T The Futile Press; 22/23 C. Varstokas; 22B Jean-Loup Charmet; 23T WFA; 23B RHPL/Jordan; 24B Zefa; 24T British Museum; 25C Zefa/Braun; 25T HPL; 25B Mick Sharp; 26T e.t. archive/ V&A; 26B DBP; 27T e.t. archive/V&A; 27B Images; 28 BAL/Bibliothèque Nationale; 29T American Museum of Natural History; 29B Environmental Picture Library; 30/31 HPL; 32B Zefa; 33T e.t. archive/New York Public Library; 33B HPL; 34/35 Panos Pictures/Penny Tweedie; 34B RHPL; 35 Panos Pictures; 36 BAL/Bristol Art Museum; 37B BAL/Bibliothèque Nationale; 37T Barnaby's; 38 e.t. archive; 39 BAL/Musée Condé; 40T Aspect/Carmichael; 40B HPL/Dorig; 41T RHPL/Beatty; 41B DBP/from Dante; 42 Patrick Wey; 43B RHPL; 43T Patrick Wey; 44 Panos Pictures/Penny Tweedie; 45T MEPL; 45B BAL/Library of Congress; 46T RHPL; 46B RHPL/Corrigan; 47T DBP; 47B Michael Holford; 48 HPL/Murray; 48/49 Michael Holford; 49 RHPL; 50 Zefa; 51T BAL/Bonhams; 51B Mary Rose Trust; 52/53 Zefa; 54T HPL/ Horner; 54B Barnaby's/Gardner; 55B Michael Holford; 55T Zefa; 56T Zefa/Thonig; 56B Arcaid; 57T e.t. archive/Biblioteca Estense; 57B Robert Estall; 58L Bath Archaeological Trust; 59T Bath Archaeological Trust; 59BC British Museum;

59BR Mansell Collection; 60 BAL/Prado; 61T Michael Holford; 61B Panos Pictures/Berriedale Johnson; 62TL HPL/Brinicombe; 62C Panos Pictures/Krofchak; 62R RHPL/Woolfitt; 63T Panos Pictures/Krofchak; 63BR Panos Pictures/ McEvoy; 64T RHPL/Gilliam; 64B BAL/British Library; 65T Zefa/Brown; 65B DBP; 66T HPL; 66B HPL/Goh; 67T BAL/Christie's; 67B Mansell Collection; 68B Rex Features/Gral/SIPA; 68T SPL/Parvainen; 69R Zefa; 69B MEPL; 70T Zefa; 71T HPL/Goh; 71B RHPL/Dukes; 72T Frank Spooner Pictures/Gamma/Gilli; 72B Rex Features/Sipa; 73 WFA/Private Collection; 74 Mick Sharp/Jean Williamson; 75T RHPL/Gervis; 75BL Rex Features/SIPA/Bean; 75BC RHPL/ Gervis; 75BR *Alone with the Past* by Richard Reed, Courtesy of the Kramer Gallery, Minneapolis; 76T HPL/McIntyre; 76B BAL/ British Library; 77B WFA/Private Collection; 77T RHPL/Woolfitt; 78T Zefa/Salmoiraghi; 78B Survival Anglia/Plage; 79T MEPL; 79B Zefa; 80L Frank Spooner/Gamma/Salaba; 80C MEPL; 80R Survival Anglia/Root; 81T MEPL; 81L Mansell Collection; 81R HPL/Frances; 82 HPL; 83T Zefa/Bundachat; 83B Zefa; 84T RHPL/Krafft; 84B RHPL; 85T RHPL/B. Lytle; 86T HPL/ Reditt; 86B Michael Holford; 87T Zefa; 88L HPL/Highet; 89T HPL/Regent; 89BR HPL/ Highet; 89BL HPL/Highet; 90 MEPL; 91 Michael Holford; 92/93 Zefa/Schorke; 94 HPL/Goh; 95 Scala; 96T HPL; 96B e.t. archive; 96T HPL; 97 WFA/Private Collection; 98 Colorphoto Hans Hinz; 99 Colorphoto Hans Hinz; 100 Robert Estall; 101T RHPL; 101B HPL/Job; 102 Dr Richard Katz; 103T FLPA/Gardener; 103B RHPL; 104 Barnaby's; 106 RHPL; 107T MEPL; 107C RHPL/Woolfitt; 107R MEPL; 108T Frank Spooner Pictures/Gamma/Jordan; 108B RHPL/ Frerck; 109 Robert Estall; 111T Ohio Historical Society; 111BL Ohio Historical Society; 111BR DBP; 113 RHPL; 114BL Tim E.H. Jones; 115T Tim E.H. Jones; 115BL Tim E.H. Jones; 116 Frank Spooner/Gamma; 117T Michael Holford; 117B Jean-Loup Charmet; 118B Mick Sharp; 119T Janet and Colin Bord; 119B Mick Sharp; 120L Mick Sharp; 121T RHPL/Woolfitt; 121BL HPL/Highet; 121BC Mick Sharp; 121BR Mick Sharp; 122L MEPL; 122C Robert Estall; 123T Zefa; 123C Mansell Collection; 124 Zefa/Mehlig; 125 RHPL/Beaumont; 126L HPL/Frances; 126R HPL/Frances; 127T Zefa/Goebel; 127BL HPL/ Lawrie; 127BC RHPL/Rennie; 127R RHPL; 128T Impact/Yann Arthus-Bertrand; 128B RHPL/